LISP PROGRAMMING

COMPUTER SCIENCE TEXTS

COMPUTER SCIENCE TEXTS

Lisp Programming

I. DANICIC
Department of Pure Mathematics,
University College of Wales

BLACKWELL SCIENTIFIC PUBLICATIONS

OXFORD LONDON EDINBURGH

BOSTON MELBOURNE

To Amanda, Sebastian and Vicky

© 1983 by
Blackwell Scientific Publications
Editorial offices:
Osney Mead, Oxford, OX2 0EL
8 John Street, London, WC1N 2ES
9 Forrest Road, Edinburgh, EH1 2QH
52 Beacon Street, Boston
  Massachusetts 02108, USA
99 Barry Street, Carlton
  Victoria 3053, Australia

First published 1983

Phototypesetting by
Parkway Illustrated Press,
Abingdon

British Library
Cataloguing in Publication Data

Danicic, I.
  Lisp programming.—(Computer science texts)
  1. Lisp (Computer program language)
  I. Title   II. Series
  001.64′24   QA76.73.L23

ISBN 0-632-01181-5

Contents

Introduction

Lisp is the second oldest computing language still in use. It has its devotees all over the world who form a somewhat 'exclusive' group. Consequently, no successful attempt has been made to standardize the language. It is probable that no two Lisps on different machines are exactly alike. The version discussed in this book is Lisp 1.5 which is the oldest and which is reasonably well documented in *LISP 1.5 Programmer's Manual* by John McCarthy *et al.* (MIT Press, 2nd ed.), subsequently referred to as the *Lisp Manual*. Anyone mastering this version should have no difficulty with any other version. Lisp has become more popular and is now available on many microcomputers.

Lisp was invented by John McCarthy to facilitate manipulations of symbolic expressions, in about 1958, and is described in outline in 'Recursive Functions of Symbolic Expressions and their Computation by Machine, Part I' by John McCarthy (*CACM*, vol. 3, No. 4, 1960). After an experimental Lisp 1, Lisp 1.5 was created at MIT, as a step towards a final version, Lisp 2, but this version never appeared. It is interesting that in those days it was expected that in future versions the notation would be radically changed, to conform more to normal mathematical usage (the so-called M-language, described briefly in the *Lisp Manual*). Fortunately, it was realized that this would have been a retrograde step as some of the strength of Lisp derives from the fact that the objects on which it operates are of exactly the same structure as the Lisp programs themselves (cf. *'History of Programming Languages*, edited by Richard L. Wexelblat, Academic Press, 1981).

Lisp is one of several so-called 'functional languages'. A conventional computer language program is conceived as consisting mainly of a sequence of commands 'first do this, then that, etc.' Lisp is quite different; a Lisp program consists of function definitions and function 'calls', i.e. requests to apply given functions to given arguments. Since most other languages also have function definitions this in itself is nothing new; it is really the lack of other types of command and apparent absence of sequences of commands that makes Lisp different in its methods.

The syntax of Lisp is very easy to learn, perhaps even easier than that of Basic, though completely different. The semantics, too, are perfectly straightforward: function calls are evaluated by evaluating the arguments and then applying the function to them. As distinct from Fortran (but not Algol and its descendants) a function can be defined in terms of itself, directly or indirectly, a facility which is often called a 'recursive definition'; such definitions are the normal method in Lisp rather than the exception and are something with which a newcomer to this language will need to become familiar. However, those to whom this idea is not new will find no difficulties here.

A question that arises is what are the purposes for which Lisp is useful, and for which is it inapplicable. It is easy to answer the second question: it is bad for 'number crunching' and elaborate printing, so one would probably not choose it for solving linear equations in many variables or for printing bank statements. It is also not suitable for text handling.

However, Lisp and other 'applicative languages' are particularly suitable for the new types of computer which are being designed now. On the traditional (von Neumann) machines, Lisp is inefficient because it demands a large computer memory and because of the sequential operation made of these computers. The new computers will have very large memories and will be able to carry out many operations at the same time, i.e. in parallel. Lisp is very suitable for such parallelism because the arguments of functions may be evaluated in parallel, and also because assignments to variables are not part of a normal Lisp program.

Lisp is particularly suitable for generating data in tree-structured form and for handling such data. Structures of this kind are appropriate in many sophisticated programming tasks; examples are: finding the best moves in games such as chess; the formal manipulation of mathematical formulae; and the organization of data such as are found in 'botanical keys' and 'expert systems'. For this reason Lisp has been successfully used for writing compilers (translators) for other computer languages, for programming robots and other artificial intelligence projects. Such programs are, of course, highly specialized, but one can equally well program in Lisp just for fun, and also for more mundane purposes. Finally, Lisp has great educational value, because it teaches one to look at computers from a different point of view.

Owing to the presence of the word LAMBDA in Lisp, some persons expect that Lisp is like Church's *Lambda Calculus*. This is not so, for the objects on which the 'Lambda Calculus' operates are so-called *lambda expressions* whereas Lisp operates on different objects, called *symbolic expressions* some of which many be regarded as *lambda expressions*, but mostly they are different.

Lisp is usually used interactively, by typing at a computer terminal and getting an immediate response from the Lisp system. This is obviously very convenient, but is by no means essential. Lisp programs can run equally well in the 'batch' mode; in this book, it is assumed, for purposes of illustration and explanation, that the user interacts with the Lisp system. This is of course essential when playing games with the computer.

The detailed examples in this book should be carefully followed. They require no specialized knowledge in any field. It will be useful if the student is familiar with an Algol-like notation as this is used for purposes of explanation. The convenient Algol 68 constructs

 if...then..else..fi

for conditionals and

 while...do...od

for loops are used as these are self-explanatory and do not require *begin...end*.

One of the drawbacks of Lisp is that it requires a lot of computer memory. If your Lisp is on a small computer you will probably not be able to run realistic programs, but you will be able to learn the language and gain the intellectual satisfaction which its use provides.

Chapter 1

Basic Lisp Notation and Functions

1.1 S-expressions

Lisp differs from conventional computer languages in many respects. The first difference is that the object on which it carries out its 'computations' are not usually numbers, but certain types of 'character strings' called 'symbolic expressions', usually abbreviated to 'S-expressions', although it can also manipulate numbers as a special case. The S-expressions are formed out of certain building blocks, called 'atoms'. Briefly, atoms *look* like identifiers in conventional languages, though their role is different. They must not contain certain 'special characters. The 'special characters' include '(' ')' '.' ',' {comma}, spaces {we regard the end of a line as a space}, and possibly some others, e.g. '10'. In addition there are 'numeric' atoms which may start with a digit, or '+' or '−', but in this case they must consist entirely of digits and perhaps a decimal point or exponent symbol E, e.g. −23 or 101 or 60.1 or 0.6E-1 {which stands for $0.6 \ 10^{-1}$}. Non-integral numbers play a very small role in Lisp and will not occur in this book. Examples of ordinary {non-numeric} atoms are: A, A1, A1, B2, LAMBDA. There is usually a limit on the number of characters in an atom, but this is quite large. S-expressions are formed according to the rules {in BNF notation}:

```
<S-expression>::=<atom>|<notatom>
<notatom>::=(<S-expression>.<S-expression>)
```

Examples of S-expressions are ABC {an atom}, (ABC . D), (A.(ABC . D)), ((A.(ABC . D)).E) {the last three are not atoms}. The last expression contains four atoms, i.e. A, ABC, D, E. It should be noted that spaces are only significant in so far as they show where an atom ends. Thus, the last S-expression above can also be written 2 ((A . (ABC.2 D)).3 E). On the other hand these spaces are not necessary since we know that dots and brackets cannot be parts of an atom.

There exist certain rules which enable one to write some S-expressions without so many brackets and dots. The main rule may be

1

stated so: We may remove from an S-expression the combination '.(' together with the corrresponding closing bracket ')' as many times as we wish. Thus

```
(A.(ABC.D))=(A ABC.D)
((A.(ABC.D)).E)=((A ABC.D).E)
(A.(B.(C.D)))=(A.(B C.D))=(A B C.D).
```

We must here be sure to introduce spaces to separate atoms from each other. It is easy to see that we can always write non-atomic S-expressions in the form $(s_1 s_2 – s_k.a)$ where the 's_j' stand for S-expressions and 'a' stands for an atom. We use '–' for an ellipsis rather than '. . .' so as to avoid any confusion with the Lisp dot. Incidentally, we may also use a comma to separate S-expressions, e.g. we can write (A(BC.D).E) as (A,(BC.D).E) and (A B C.D) as (A,B,C.D). An end of a line is also treated as a space. There is a further abbreviation possible. For this purpose the special atom NIL is introduced. The S-expression $(s_1 s_2 – s_k.NIL)$ is called a *list* and may be written $(s_1 s_2 – s_k)$, thus eliminating the solitary dot. Thus

```
((A.B)(C.D)E.NIL)=((A.B)(C.D)E)
```

The s_i in the list $(s_1 s_2 – s_k)$ are called its elements. They can of course be arbitrary S-expressions. Since lists are easier to write than general S-expressions it is usual to use them whenever this seems natural. Expressions with dots usually appear as 'association lists of pairs', e.g.

```
((A.X)((B C).Y)(E.Z))
```

Since (s) stands for $(s.NIL)$ one can by analogy also write ( ) for NIL. This makes NIL the only atom which is also a list. It represents the list without elements, i.e. the empty list. Thus $((( )))=$ ((NIL))=((NIL).NIL)=((NIL.NIL).NIL).

We have now explained all the rules for abbreviating S-expressions. The unpractised reader should practise going from non-abbreviated S-expressions to the fully abbreviated forms, and back again in a systematic way. The fully 'dotted' expression gives a better idea of the structure of the expression. The list of atoms (A B C D), when written in this form, is simple but misleading, since it is in fact far from symmetric. This becomes clear if it is written as (A.(B.(C.(D.NIL)))).

Two S-expressions are equal if, and only if, when written in fully non-abbreviated form they are identical except for spaces, which are ignored, atoms being equal only if they are 'spelled' identically.

A most useful technique of checking the correctness of an S-expression is that of 'bracket-counting'. An arbitrary integer b {=bracket count} is chosen and, moving from left to right along the S-expression S, when '(' is encountered b is written down immediately before the '(' {or above it} and then b is increased by 1. Whenever ')' is encountered b is decreased by 1 and {the new} b is written down to the right of ')' {or above it}. Thus taking $b=0$ initially, we get

```
0( 1(A.B)1 1(C.D)1 E)0
```

and for a typical S-expression occurring in a Lisp program {cf. Fig. 2}, the following:

```
0(IF 1(LAMBDA 2(D)2 2(COND 3(4(NULL R)4 NIL)3
   3(4(ATOM R)4 4(PSP 5(PR 6(PDOT NIL)6)5)4)3
   3(T 4(MU 5(CAR R)5 5(DOR R)5)4)3
   )2)1)0
```

In this way we can see where any sub S-expression begins and ends. An S-expression starting with bracket-count b, e.g. '2(' ends with the first bracket to its right which has the same b attached to it, e.g. ')2' {we shall say that such an S-expression has bracket count b}. In the above example the sub S-expression starting '2(COND' in the first line ends with the first bracket in the fourth line and the S-expression starting '3(T' in the third line ends at the end of that line. We also see that the whole S-expression is a list with two elements of the form

```
(IF s)
```

s being the long S-expression starting '1(LAMBDA' and ending ')1' in the fourth line. A Lisp system should contain a bracket-counting program, but in any case bracket counting should be done by hand during the writing of a program. In this book most S-expressions will have bracket-counting numbers placed above the brackets as an aid to the readers. In an actual program these numbers must of course be absent.

Figure 1 shows an actual Lisp computation as seen on a computer terminal {the details will of course vary in different implementations}. The '*' is printed by the computer to show that it requires the user to type something. The first line is a request for Lisp to use the file 'HANOIBK' instead of the terminal. When the computer is ready to print something, it first prints '⇒'. The effect of the 'LOAD' {which is not standard Lisp} is that the system reads from the file, but prints at the

```
*LISP


* LOAD((QUOTE HANOIBK))
==>
(MOVE MOVE1 MOVE2 WR HANOI)

NIL
* HANOI(4)
==>

MOVE 1 TO 3
MOVE 1 TO 2
MOVE 3 TO 2
MOVE 1 TO 3
MOVE 2 TO 1
MOVE 2 TO 3
MOVE 1 TO 3
MOVE 1 TO 2
MOVE 3 TO 2
MOVE 3 TO 1
MOVE 2 TO 1
MOVE 3 TO 2
MOVE 1 TO 3
MOVE 1 TO 2
MOVE 3 TO 2
NIL
* DONE
*LIST HANOIBK

DEFINE((
(MOVE(LAMBDA(N A B C) (COND
                      ((ZEROP N)(TERPRI))
                      (T(MOVE2(WR(MOVE1)))))))
(MOVE1(LAMBDA()MOVE(SUB1 N)A C B)))
(MOVE2(LAMBDA(D)(MOVE(SUB1 N)C B A)))
(WR(LAMBDA(D)(AND(PRIN1 BLANK)
                 (PRIN1 A)
                 (PRIN1 BLANK)
                 (PRIN1(QUOTE TO))
                 (PRIN1 BLANK)
                 (PRIN1 B)
)  )          )
(HANOI(LAMBDA(N)(MOVE N 1 2 3)))
))


*
```

Fig. 1

```
 DEFINE
((
(PSP(LAMBDA(D)(PRIN1 BLANK)))
(PDOT(LAMBDA(D)(PRIN1 PERIOD)))
(PR (LAMBDA(D)(PRIN1 R)))
(PRNUM (LAMBDA(D)(PRIN1 BC)))
(PLPAR(LAMBDA(D)(PRIN1 LPAR)))
(PRPAR(LAMBDA(D)(PRIN1 RPAR)))
(MU (LAMBDA(L R)(IF(ANALYSE L (ADD1 BC)))))
(IF (LAMBDA(D) (COND ((NULL R) NIL)
                     ((ATOM R) (PSP(PR(PDOT NIL))))
                 (T (MU (CAR R) (CDR R)))
             )))
(ANALYSE (LAMBDA(X BC)(COND
((ATOM X) (PSP(PRIN1 X)))
                  (T (PSP(PRNUM(PRPAR(MUX(PLPAR
                                          (PRNUM T))))))))
)))
(MU (LAMBDA(D) (MU (CAR X) (CDR X))))
(CHECK (LAMBDA(X)(ANALYSE X 0)))
          ))
DEFINE
((
(IF1(LAMBDA(Y)(COND
    ((EQ Y $EOF$)(QUOTE DONE))
    (T(OR(TERPRI)(FILECHECK(ANALYSE Y 0))))
)))
(FILECHECK(LAMBDA(D)(IF1(READ))))
(FILECOUNT(LAMBDA(N)(FILECHECK(RDS N))))
))
OPENR(1 MYFILE21)
FILECOUNT(1)
DONE
```

Fig. 2

terminal. When it has finished with the file it expects further typing at the terminal. In this case it prints

```
(MOVE MOVE1 MOVE2 WR HANOI)
```

because this is the only printing it was required to do when executing the commands in the file 'HANOIBK'. The user typed 'HANOI(4)' and the Lisp system executes this function call as shown, giving the moves required for solving the 'towers of Hanoi' puzzle with four discs. When the user types 'DONE' he leaves the Lisp system. There follows a request to print the file {'LIST HANOIBK'} and this is shown. The details of this program will be discussed later.

1.2 Functions and forms

In Lisp there are only functions and functions applied to arguments {'calls'} and these must be carefully distinguished from each other. A function is exactly like an Algol procedure which yields a value {e.g. like integer procedure} and usually has formal parameters. Every function in Lisp must yield {'return'} some value. A function call is called a 'form' in Lisp. These look different from the more usual function calls because they are S-expressions. Thus if $F1$ is a function of two variables, a call in most computer languages would look like this:

$F1(a,b)$.

The corresponding form in Lisp is

```
(F1 A B)
```

which is a list of three elements. It could of course be written (F1,A,B) or (F1 A B.Nil) or (F1.(A.(B.NIL))). Suppose F2 and F3 are functions of one variable. The usual call $F1(F2(c),F3(d))$ has the following form in Lisp:

```
(F1(F2 C)(F3 D))
```

and so on. The general rule should be quite clear from this. The atoms C,D above, i.e. the 'actual parameters', are also regarded as forms. Formally, a definition of *form* and related concepts is {in BNF notation}:

```
<form>::=(<function><args>)|<atom>|<special
                           form>|(<form><args>)
```

```
<arg>::=<form>|(FUNCTION<function>)|
<args>::=<empty>|<arg><args>
<special form>::=(QUOTE<S-expression>)| (COND<pairs>)
<pair>::=(<form><form>)
<pairs>::=<pair>|<pair><pairs>
<empty>::=
```

For example in Section 1.1 {cf. Fig. 2} there occurs a <special form> of type (COND<pairs>) in which there are three pairs each beginning and ending with bracket-count 3. The form itself has bracket-count 2. The whole S-expression {with bracket-count 0} is an example of a <pair>. The third <pair> has as its second member the form

(MU(CAR R)(CDR R))

Here , MU, CAR, CDR are functions; the actual parameters for the function MU are the forms (CAR R) and (CDR R). This is an example of <form>::=(<function><args>) with <args> =(CAR R)(CDR R). Thus MU must be a function of two arguments, CAR and CDR functions of one argument. Arguments are also called parameters.

Functions usually have names, such as MU, CAR, CDR above and are therefore atoms. They can also be represented by an S-expression of type

(LAMDA(X–Z)<form>).

This is exactly analogous to a routine text in Algol 68. The <form> is the 'body' of the function and LAMBDA(X Y) introduces the formal parameters X,Y. These can be any non-numerical atoms. The analogy with Algol 68 goes further in that the function (LAMBDA–) need not be given a name but is a legitimate function just by itself. The syntax for functions is:

```
<function>::=<non-numerical atom>|<λ-expression>
            (LABEL<name><λ-expression>)
<λ-expression>::=(LAMBDA(<vars>)<form>)
<var>::=<non-numerical atom>
<vars>::=empty|<var><vars>
<name>::=<non-numerical atom>
```

An example of a <λ-expression> is the expression in Fig. 1 starting (LAMBDA(D), having bracket-count 1. The corresponding <form>, i.e. the 'body' starts with (COND and has bracket-count 2. The

$<\lambda$-expression$>$ here is a function of one variable, the variable or formal parameter being 'D'. We have now explained all the Lisp syntax; clearly it is extremely simple and will easily be memorized with some practice.

1.3 Initial functions

In Lisp there are five primitive functions: CAR, CDR, CONS, ATOM, EQ. These will be recognized automatically by the Lisp system. In principle, they are sufficient for any computation in Lisp, any other functions being defined by the user in terms of these, though in practice a Lisp system usually recognizes by name many other functions as well. The action of functions can best be explained by using conventional, functional, rather than Lisp, notation, with the use of '[' and ']', instead of round brackets in order to avoid confusion with the brackets of S-expressions. Thus if $f1$ is a function we denote by $f1[a]$ or $f1[a,b]$, and the usual $f1(a), f1(a,b)$ if s_1 and s_2 are arbitrary S-expressions

    CAR[(s₁.s₂)] = s₁,
    CDR[(s₁.s₂)] = s₂.

CAR and CDR are undefined if the argument is an atom,

    CONS[s₁,s₂] = (s₁.s₂) .

Examples of these three functions are as follows:

    CAR[(A.B)] = A
    CDR[(A.B)] = B
    CAR[(A)] = A
    CDR[(A)] = NIL
    CONS[A,B] = (A.B)
    CONS[A,NIL] = (A)
    CONS[(A B),(C D)] = ((A B).(C D))
                       = ((A B)C D)
    CONS[A,(B C D E)] = (A B C D E)
    CONS(A,(B C D.E)] = (A B C D.E)

The remaining two functions are 'predicates', i.e. they yield only two values, generally called true and false. In Lisp 'true' is represented by the special atom*T* and false is represented by our familiar NIL, for reasons of convenience to be explained later.

For atoms a,b

    EQ[a,b] is *T* if a = b, NIL otherwise.

Thus

```
EQ[A,A] = *T*
EQ[UV,UV] = *T*
EQ[A,B] = NIL.
```

EQ may not work for numeric atoms. In that case 'EQUAL' should be used. This is the original definition of EQ but for convenience it is extended to the cases EQ[a,b] where at least one of a,b is an atom, with the obvious meaning:

```
EQ[a,b] = NIL if exactly one of a,b is not an atom.
```

To test for equality of any S-expressions the predicate EQUAL is used. It can be defined in terms of the primitive functions. The predicate ATOM is defined to be true if its argument is an atom, false otherwise:

```
ATOM[s] = *T* if s is an atom, NIL otherwise.
```

For example,

```
ATOM[ABC] = *T*, ATOM[3] = *T*,
ATOM[(A B C)] = NIL.
```

To avoid misunderstanding, note that the above examples are not Lisp fragments, as is emphasized by the square brackets; they merely serve to explain the particular functions.

Chapter 2

Simple Programming

2.1 The top level*

A Lisp program has the following structure:

$$fn_1 \ \text{list}_1$$
$$fn_2 \ \text{list}_2$$

$$\cdot \ \cdot \ \cdot$$
$$\cdot \ \cdot \ \cdot$$
$$\cdot \ \cdot \ \cdot$$

$$fn_k \ \text{list}_k$$

where each *fn* is an S-expression representing a function as explained in Chapter 1 and each list is of the form

$$(\text{arg}_1\text{–arg}_m)$$

where arg_j is an S-expression, the jth actual argument for the function in question. *These arguments are not evaluated in any way.* Here is such a program:

```
CAR((A B C))
CAR((A))
CDR((B))
CONS(A (B C))
CONS(A B)
```

It is convenient to call each of these pairs of S-expressions a 'top-level pair'. It is usual to program Lisp in an interactive mode though this need not be so. For clarity I shall assume that we type in the program. It is then probably usual that after typing in a top-level pair we press the carriage return key. Having done this the computer will print the result. The computer always prints S-expressions in the fully abbreviated form but will of course accept any of the legal forms of S-expression. In the example above the computer will respond, following each pair, with A,

---

* Before reading this chapter please consult Section 10.4 concerning superficially different Lisp Systems.

A, NIL, (A B C), (A.B) respectively. The beginner might now be tempted to type

    CAR((CONS(A B)))

hoping to get the computer to print A. Instead, to his surprise, it will print

    CONS   !

If you think about this it is not really surprising, because the structure of CAR((CONS(A B))) is exactly the same as that of CAR((C(A B))) which one expects to produce C. Worse would happen if we typed

    CAR(CONS(A B))

which will probably produce some error message because CAR is a function of one variable and we are presenting it here with two actual parameters, CONS and (A B). So how do we tell the computer to use the compound function CAR CONS? Here we need a λ-expression. This function is represented by

    (LAMBDA(X,Y)(CAR(CONS X Y)))

so if we type

```
    0        1    11   2        2100   0
    (LAMBDA(X,Y)(CAR(CONS X Y)))(A B)
```

the computer will respond:

    A

Similarly, the top-level pair

```
    0       1    11    2      22      210
    (LAMBDA(XX Y)(CONS(CAR XX)(CDR Y)))
    01   11   10
    ((A B)(C D))
```

produces the response

    (A D)

A form which represents a call is evaluated in the usual way: the actual parameters are evaluated and then the function is applied to them. {This is usually called evaluation by value}. If the function in question is represented by a formal parameter of some other function then the corresponding actual parameter, which must be a function, is submitted for the formal parameter and the form is evaluated with this function. Thus, if the form is, say (CONS X Y) {corresponding to a call

CONS[X,Y]} then X,Y are evaluated and the function CONS is applied to the result. If the form is

```
(W X Y)
```

where W is not a function known to the system it will be expected that the variable W is the formal parameter of some function and that the corresponding actual parameter, a function e.g. CONS or (LAMBDA(Z_1 Z_2)(CONS Z_1(CDR Z_2))), is to be used in place of W. More generally the function may be represented by a form which on evaluation yields a function. This evaluation will be performed; examples of this will be given in Chapter 7.

2.2   The special forms

The form (QUOTE<S-expression>) yields on evaluation the corresponding <S-expression> e.g.

```
(QUOTE Z)
```

yields Z and

```
(QUOTE(LAMBDA(X)X))
```

yields (LAMBDA(X)X).

The special form

```
(COND(a₁ e₁)(a₂ e₂)—(aₖ eₖ))
```

corresponds to the usual

```
if  a₁ then  e₁
else if  a₂ then  e₂
 . . .
 . . .
 . . .
else if  aₖ then  eₖ
fi
```

The forms a_i are evaluated from left to right until one is found which is 'true' and then the corresponding form e is evaluated and its value is the yield of the COND form. If none of the a_i are true then an error message should be obtained. Since 'true' is denoted by the atom *T* and 'false' by NIL it might be expected that the yields of the a_i should be *T* or NIL. In fact this is not necessary; for convenience, any value which is not NIL is regarded as 'true'. Thus we can write the form

```
(COND((CAR X)Y)
((CDR X)Z))
```

which will yield the value of Y if CAR[X] is not NIL; but if CAR[X] is NIL then it will yield the value of Z provided that CDR[X] is not NIL; in all other cases an error will result. Thus if X represents (A) the yield is {the value of} Y but if X represents (NIL.A) then the yield is {the value of} Z. If X is (NIL), an error will result. Note, incidentally, that neither COND nor QUOTE are functions. Thus we cannot write at the top level QUOTE((A B C)).

If n is a number we do not need to write (QUOTE n) since n can only stand for itself.

2.3 The function CSET

This function does roughly the same as an 'assignment' in conventional languages. Thus, if we write at the top level

```
CSET(COLOURS(RED YELLOW BLUE))
```

then the list (RED YELLOW BLUE) will be associated with the atom COLOURS and this will be reflected by the fact that when COLOURS occurs where a form is expected, it will yield on evaluation the list (RED YELLOW BLUE), e.g. the top level pair

```
 0       1 1        00 0
(LAMBDA( )COLOURS)( )
```

will produce (RED YELLOW BLUE).

This also provides an example of a function of no variables. The corresponding call at an inner level would be the form

```
 0 1     2 2         1 0
((LAMBDA( )COLOURS))
```

The reader should carefully think out the reason for the extra pair of brackets, with reference to the general appearance of forms representing calls.

The first parameter of CSET must represent an atom, the second may be any S-expression. The yield of CSET[a,b] is b {in some implementations the yield is (b) or even a} and then the atom a is said to have APVAL {standing for 'applied value'} b. a retains this APVAL until it is given a new one by another CSET.

The only possibilities for an atom to act as a form are: (i) if it is the formal parameter of some function, in which case it will yield the value of the corresponding actual parameter; (ii) if it has been given an APVAL, in which case it will yield the corresponding value; and (iii) if it is a numerical atom, in which case its yield is the corresponding number.

For these three reasons, an atom that has been given an APVAL must never be used as a formal parameter of a function and vice-versa. It is therefore very desirable to distinguish atoms with APVALs in some special way. Here we shall incorporate the symbol '%' in such atoms, e.g. COLOUR%. Obviously a numerical atom cannot be used for any purpose other than that of representing a number.

2.4   The function DEFINE

This is a function of one variable. Its purpose is to give names to functions. The actual parameter of DEFINE is a list of type

$$((a_1\ f_1)-(a_n\ f_n))$$

where the a_i are atoms and the f_i, S-expressions representing functions. The yield of

$$\texttt{DEFINE[}((a_1 f_1)-(a_n f_n))\texttt{]}$$

is the list $(a_1\ a_2-a_n)$ but the important thing is the side-effect that it associates the function f_i with the atom a_i. As a result, whenever a form contains the atom a_i in a place where a function is expected the function f_i will be used. This association can be changed by a new DEFINE.

The following is an example of the function DEFINE:

```
DEFINE((
  (HEAD CAR)
  (TAIL CDR)
  (COMBINE CONS)
))
```

Note the brackets '((' after DEFINE and '))' at the end. This layout is usually used. The first bracket is the bracket for 'list of arguments', always present at the top level. The second bracket is the beginning of the single actual parameter, i.e. the list of pairs. In this example it is a list of three pairs. After having defined the functions HEAD, TAIL and COMBINE we can use them whenever we wish instead of CAR, CDR, CONS respectively. Here is a complete program showing the various features so far discussed. Brackets '{ }' will be used for comments; they and their contents are not part of the program. '→' indicates the computer response. {If EQ does not work for numbers then EQUAL should be used below.}

```
        0 1
DEFINE((
    2   3       4   44      5       5432
    (REP(LAMBDA(X Y)(CONS X(CDR Y))))
    2        3       4   44
    (REPLACE(LAMBDA(X N)(COND
    5 6     66   7        7 65
    ((EQ N 1)(REP(CAR COLOURS%)X))
    5 6     66   7    8        87 65
    ((EQ N 2)(REP(CAR(CDR COLOURS%))X))
    5 6     66   7
    ((EQ N 3)(REP(CAR
      8    9              987 65
      (CDR(CDR COLOURS%)))X))
    432
    )))
10
))
```

→ (REP REPLACE)   *{The order in which the functions are defined within DEFINE is immaterial}*

CSET(COLOURS%(RED GREEN))   *{COLOURS% now has an APVAL}*

→ (RED GREEN)
REPLACE((BLACK BLUE)2)
→ (GREEN BLUE)
REPLACE((THIS IS GOOD)1)
→ (RED IS GOOD)
CSET(COLOURS%(GREEN AMBER RED))
→ (GREEN AMBER RED)   *{COLOURS% now has a new APVAL}*

REPLACE((MY SPECTACLES ARE DIRTY)3)
→ (RED SPECTACLES ARE DIRTY)
REPLACE(COLOURS% 2)
→ ERROR   *{some further messages might follow indicating that an attempt was made to evaluate CDR of atom COLOURS%, or, more likely, no error indication results but gibberish is printed}*

(LAMBDA()(REPLACE COLOURS% 2))()
→ (AMBER AMBER RED)
(LAMBDA()COLOURS%)()
→ (GREEN AMBER RED)   *{end of program}*

The function REPLACE as defined in this program acts on an S-expression X and integer N, replacing the CAR of X by the Nth (where N=1,2,3) member of the APVAL of COLOURS%. In the last but one call the yield of COLOURS% has been taken as this X. The last call shows that this has not affected the APVAL of COLOURS%.

2.5 F-functions, built-in functions and APVALS

In principle, all Lisp programming could be done with the means described so far, apart from 'reading' and 'printing' {input and output}, and functions as arguments which will be described later. For convenience every Lisp system offers the user many other functions such as LIST, APPEND, EQUAL, ADD, LESSP, AND, OR, CSETQ, DEFLIST, EVAL, APPLY etc. which are described in Appendix 2, though not all described there will be available or even relevant, and many others not described there will be supplied by each Lisp system according to the tastes of the implementers and the users. There will also be built-in atoms having APVALs among which will certainly be T with APVAL *T* {or in some systems T} and NIL with APVAL NIL {sic} and probably F with APVAL NIL. Since NIL has APVAL NIL there is never a need to write (QUOTE NIL). If F {which stands for 'false'} is not present and the programmer wishes to have it, he only needs to type CSET (F NIL) to get it. Most of the built-in functions will be ordinary functions which the user could define himself, but there are some exceptions. An example of an exceptional function is LIST in that it has as many arguments as the programmer wants. Thus the form

    (LIST X)

is equivalent to (CONS X NIL) and

    (LIST X Y Z)

is equivalent to (CONS X(CONS Y(CONS Z NIL))).

In the first case LIST behaves as a function of one variable and in the second as a function of three variables. This makes programming easier. In all other respects LIST behaves like an ordinary function. Another function of this type is PLUS.

Here, functions of this type will be called F-functions. Among these are AND, OR and CSETQ. They enable one to cheat the Lisp syntax and semantics in order to get more concise programs. Take for instance CSETQ. This is a function of two variables and is like CSET but differs from it in that its first argument is not evaluated. This means that instead of writing the form

    (CSET(QUOTE TAX%)Z)

we can write more concisely

    (CSETQ TAX% Z).

On the other hand we must not use CSETQ at the top level in the normal way as this would be meaningless. Thus the top level pair

    CSETQ(A%(B C.D))

should give an error message.

The function AND is a 'function' of as many variables as desired {like LIST} but it also has another property, i.e. some of its arguments may not be evaluated, depending on the values of other arguments. If s_1–s_n stand for arbitrary S-expressions then the call AND $[s_1$–$s_n]$ is evaluated by first evaluating s_1. If the value is NIL, then evaluation stops {and the yield is NIL} otherwise s_2 is evaluated and so on. Evaluation of arguments stops as soon as a value NIL is met. The yield is *T* if none has value NIL. Thus the form

    (AND F1 F2 F3)

is equivalent to the form

$$\overset{0}{(}\text{COND}\overset{1}{(}\overset{2}{(}\text{NULL } \text{F1}\overset{2}{)}\text{NIL}\overset{1}{)}\overset{1}{(}\overset{2}{(}\text{NULL } \text{F2}\overset{2}{)}\text{NIL}\overset{1}{)}\overset{1}{(}\overset{2}{(}\text{NULL } \text{F3}\overset{2}{)}\text{NIL}\overset{1}{)}\overset{1}{(}\text{T } \text{T}\overset{1}{)}\overset{0}{)}.$$

OR $[s_1$–$s_n]$ is similar except that evaluating stops as soon as a non-NIL value is found

In the *Lisp Manual* and elsewhere the built-in F-functions are listed and can be recognized because they have the type FSUBR or FEXPR. They are not usually used at the top level, but for completeness the following rule for using them at the top level should be noted: if FF is an F-function of one variable and *arg* is a form then the top level pair

    FF(arg)

is evaluated in the same way as the form

    (FF arg),

at an inner level, and similarly for F-functions of several variables.

The following is an example of the above: after

    CSET(A% (U.V))

the pair

```
CSETQ(B% A%))
```

will give the APVAL

```
(U.V) to B%
```

and the pair

```
OR(A% NIL)
```

will yield *T*.

Finally, various combinations of CAR and CDR often occur in programs so a special notation may be used for these, e.g. the function

```
(LAMBDA(X)(CAR(CDR(CAR X))))
```

is denoted by CADAR, and

```
(LAMBDA(X)(CDR(CAR X)))
```

by CDAR, etc. In general, such combinations are denoted by C--R where the dashes are replaced by any number of A's and D's, with an obvious meaning. Many of these many be expected to be built-in in every Lisp system.

Chapter 3

Programming Methods

3.1 Iteration

Programs written in any of the conventional computing languages usually rely on various types of loop constructs to carry out repetitive computations, for example,

    for J to N *do* .... *od*
or   *for* J to N *while* ... *do* .... *od.*

Lisp does not have these facilities, or rather, different implementations offer various loop facilities, such as the PROG feature briefly described in Section 10.6; these are, however, usually ill-defined and really not in accordance with the spirit of Lisp. The reason why they are offered is said to be greater efficiency but the real intention is probably to make Lisp more acceptable to the casual user.

In Lisp, loops of all kinds are achieved by means of 'recursive functions', that is functions in whose definition occur calls on the function being defined; such calls may also be indirect via a chain of calls which eventually lead to calls on the function being defined. The reader may well be used to this already, since the same may be done in many other languages. In fact, it is hoped that, with a little practice, writing recursive functions will be found simpler than using conventional loops; and in some cases, it should be noted, it is almost impossible to find suitable loops to replace recursive functions.

As a simple example, let us define a function CDNR such that for positive integer N and S-expression s CDNR[N,s] is CDR[CDR—[CDR[s]]—], CDR being applied N times, provided that this has a meaning. It also seems natural to define CDNR[0,s] as s. The informal recursive definition we easily obtain is

CDNR[N,s]::=*if* N=0 *then* s
                else
                    CDR[CDNR[N—1,s]]
          fi.

Here '::=' means something like 'is defined as'; we shall often use this type of notation in the hope that it will help the reader. In Lisp this is

```
         0 1
DEFINE((

    2       3        4     5 4 4
    (CDNR(LAMBDA(N  S)(COND
        5 6          6    5
        ((ZEROP  N)  S)
        5    6    7       8          8  7 6 5
        (T  (CDR(CDNR(SUB1  N)S))))
    4 3 2
    )))
  1 0
))
```

Here ZEROP and SUB1 are standard functions. The ending 'P' in a function name usually indicates a predicate. Obviously, then, ZEROP[N] =*T* if N=0, NIL otherwise. SUB1 [N]=N−1. Note the use of T in place of 'else'. It could be replaced by any form which does not yield NIL and whose evaluation has no side effects. We can use the CDNR function to redefine the function REPLACE of Section 2.4, so as to make it applicable for all N instead of only for N ≤ 3. Thus {omitting, as we often shall, 'DEFINE((' and the corresponding ')')'}:

```
   0          1      2     2 2
  (REPLACE(LAMBDA(X  N)(REP
     3    4     5       5          4 3  2
    (CAR(CDNR(SUB1  N)COLOURS%))X)
  1 0
))
```

The atom REP could of course be replaced by

```
(LAMBDA(Z  Y)  (CONS  Z(CDR  Y)))
```

or even by

```
(LAMBDA(X  Y)(CONS  X(CDR  Y)))
```

as the Lisp system will not confuse the two variables X but the reader might, so it is best to avoid such clashes of names of variables.

Let us now consider a more typical case. The standard function REVERSE has the following effect when applied to a list:

$$\text{REVERSE}[(s_1 s_2 – s_n)] = (s_n s_{n-1} – s_1)$$
and   REVERSE[NIL]=NIL;

it is not defined for S-expressions which are not lists. In the *Lisp Manual* this is described (in a different notation) as follows:

```
REVERSE[L]::=u:=L; v:=NIL;
            while u ≠ NIL do
            v:=CONS[CAR[u],v];
            u:=CDR[u]
                              od;
            yield v.
```

Here u and v are supposed to be variables. Although Lisp has the concept of assignments to variables, using CSET, there is no concept of a local variable created in the body of a function to which assignments may be made. All such variables are global, such as the COLOURS% example given previously. Assignments of the above kind are therefore avoided in Lisp. Let us rewrite the above thus:

```
REVERSE[L]::=WHL[L,NIL]
WHL[U,V]::=while U ≠ NIL do
              etc.
                            od;
              yield v.
```

As it stands the WHL function does not make sense because it contains assignments to its formal parameters. Let us rewrite WHL in such a way as to bring out the meaning of the *while* loop:

```
WHL[U,V]::=if U ≠ NIL then
              yield WHL[CDR[U],CONS[CAR[U],V]]
              else yield V
              fi
```

This is now free of assignements and is immediately translatable into Lisp:

```
 0        1      2  22        210
(REVERSE(LAMBDA(L)(WHL  L  NIL)))
 0    1      2   22
(WHL(LAMBDA(U  V)(COND
   3 4    5      55      6        6 543
  (U(WHL(CDR  U)(CONS(CAR  U)V)))
   3   3
  (T  V)
 210
)))
```

Here is a more complicated example. The function REV is applicable to a list $(s_1 s_2 - s_n)$ where each s_i is an atom or a list of this type and $REV[(s_1 s_2 - s_n)] = (REV[s_n]REV[s_{n-1}] - REV[s_1])$, i.e. in the words of the *Lisp Manual*, REV reverses a list and all its sublists. Since some or all s_i

can be atoms, we mean by the above notation that $REV[s]=s$ if s is an atom. We note that $REV[(s_1-s_n)]$ may be obtained in two stages. First form $(REV[s_1]-REV[s_n])$ and then apply REVERSE to this. This gives

```
REV[L]::=REVERSE[REV2[L]]
REV2[S]::=if ATOM[S] then yield S
          else
          yield CONS[REV[CAR[S]],REV2[CDR[S]]]
          fi   {REV2[(s₁-sₙ)]=(REV[s₁]-REV[sₙ])}
```

and this at once translates into Lisp thus:

```
 0   1        2 22        3        3210
(REV(LAMBDA(L)(REVERSE(REV2 L))))
 0    1       2 22
(REV2(LAMBDA(S)(COND
   34     4 3
  ((ATOM S)S)
   3 4   5      6       655    6        6543
  (T(CONS(REV(CAR S))(REV2(CDR S)))))
210
)))
```

Note that REV calls REV2 and REV2 calls itself as well as REV, quite a sophisticated example of 'mutual recursion'. These examples should be studied until thoroughly understood. The reader might like to think up other similar examples and to give different definitions. For instance REVERSE could be defined using the function APPEND. If l_1 and l_2 are lists then $APPEND[l_1,l_2]$ makes a single list by 'appending' l_2 to l_1, so if $l_1 = (x_1-x_m)$, $l_2 = (y_1-y_n)$ then $APPEND[l_1, l_2] = (x_1-x_my_1-y_n)$. The beginner often confuses this with $CONS[l_1,l_2]$ which is quite a different object:

$$CONS[l_1,l_2]=((x_1-x_m).(y_1-y_n))$$
$$=((x_1-x_m)\ y_1-y_n)$$

and no further abbreviation is possible.

Now $REVERSE[l]$ could be defined by appending $CONS[CAR[l],NIL]$ to $REVERSE[CDR[l]]$ (unless $l=NIL$). Note that $CONS[CAR[l],NIL]$ is more simply written $LIST[CAR[l]]$. The reader should try this as an exercise.

As an illustration, let us write a program which shows how to solve the puzzle 'towers of Hanoi'. This puzzle consists of three vertical pegs, on one of which are placed a certain number of discs with a hole in the centre {usually five}, all of different size, the biggest being at the bottom, the others being on top of this one in order of decreasing size. The object is to transfer all the discs to another peg without ever placing a disc on top of a smaller one. One can move only one disc at a time. There is essentially only one way of doing it: to move the discs from peg A to peg B, move all but the bottom one to the third peg C, move the remaining {largest} disc from A to B and then move the discs from C to B {without moving the biggest disc again}. This statement gives a 'recursive' definition, since we need to know how to move n discs before we can move $n+1$ discs. The method required 2^n-1 moves for n discs {and this is best possible}.

Let us suppose that move $[n,a,b,c]$ tells us how to move n discs from peg a to peg b. The above can then be expressed so:

```
move[n,a,b,c]::=if n=0 then print a new line else
                                      move[n−1,a,c,b];
                     print:'MOVE' a 'to' b;
                     move(n−1,c,b,a]
                     fi
```

In Lisp these three calls on the right are the forms

```
 0        1      1    0
(MOVE(SUB1    n)A C B),
 0    1        2        2 1
(AND(PRIN1(QUOTE  MOVE))
       1        1
      (PRIN1 BLANK)
       1    1
      (PRIN1 A)
       1        1
      (PRIN1 BLANK)
       1    2      2 1
      (PRIN1(QUOTE  TO))
       1    1
      (PRIN1 B)
 0
)
 0        1    1  0
(MOVE(SUB1 N)C B A)
```

PRIN1 prints only an atom and does not move the printer to the next line. It yields the S-expression printed. BLANK has an APVAL which on printing prints a space.

In the next section we shall learn how to complete writing this program.

3.2 Programming successive commands

Conventional programs usually include a number of 'successive statements'

$$S_1; S_2; -$$

which means, first do S_1, then S_2, etc. In Lisp this does not occur as frequently but can be done by means of a 'dummy variable'. Corresponding to the statements S_1, S_2 we have Lisp forms. Suppose f_1 and f_2 are forms and we wish to evaluate f_1 and then f_2

Let us define a function G2 thus:

```
(G2(LAMBDA(D)f₂))
```

where D is an atom not occuring in f_2. The evaluation of the form

```
(G2 f₁)
```

does precisely what is required. f_1 is evaluated first and then G2 is applied to this value which means that f_2 is evaluated. Similarly if we wanted to evaluate f_1, then f_2 and next f_3 we introduce the function G3:

```
(G3(LAMBDA(D)f₃))
```

and make the call

```
(G3(G2 f₁)).
```

We could of course replace G2 {and G3} by the corresponding lambda-expressions, but this can get quite unwieldy, e.g.

```
((LAMBDA(D)f₂)f₁)
```

especially if the forms f_j are complicated. This method may be used for any number of forms f_j. The important thing is that the dummy variable, such as D above, does not occur in the corresponding form.

For example, in the 'towers of Hanoi' puzzle of Section 3.1 the three forms which are to be evaluated successively are made into functions; the first one becomes a function of no arguments:

```
(MOVE1(LAMBDA()(MOVE(SUB1 N)A C B)))
```

The second and third become functions of one dummy variable:

```
(MOVE2(LAMBDA(D)(MOVE(SUB1 N)C B A)))
```

and

```
(WR(LAMBDA(D)(AND(PRINT1(QUOTE MOVE))
```

```
            (PRIN1 BLANK)
            (PRIN1 A)
            (PRIN1 BLANK)
            (PRIN1 (QUOTE TO))
            (PRIN1 BLANK)
            (PRIN1 B)
)))
```

and these are put together in the functions MOVE:

```
 0       1       2       2 2
(MOVE(LAMBDA(N A B C)(COND
   3 4        4 4       4 3
  ((ZEROP N)(TERPRI))
   3 4      5   6    6 5 4 3 2 1 0
  (T(MOVE2(WR(MOVE1)))))))
```

Incidentally TERPRI is a function of no argument; it prints a new line.

The bracket-counting program of Fig. 2 provides another good example of this and other Lisp features, so let us turn to it (cf. p. 5).

The program reads any S-expression and prints out the expression in fully abbreviated form together with the corresponding bracket numbers.

Let x be the S-expression and bc the current bracket count and let ANALYSE[x,bc] be the function which does all this. If x is not an atom then $x = (l.r)$ where l and r are S-expressions. In fully abbreviated form $x = (lr_1-r_k.a)$ or (lr_1-r_k) if the atom a is NIL.

Thus we want

print(bc);print('(');analyse(l,bc+1);analyse(r_1,bc+1)
etc. up to analyse(r_k,bc+1). Then if a is not NIL,
print('.') and print (a). Finally print (')'); print
(bc).

Let MU[l,r] be the function that deals with l,r_1-r_k,a. From this we get, with a little effort

```
MU[l,r]::=ANALYSE[l,bc+1];
  if null[r]  then NIL        {this value is unimportant}
  else if atom [r]  then
    print ('.') print [r]; print [' ']
    else MU[car[r],cdr[r]]
  fi
fi
```

The main function ANALYSE can be defined by

ANALYSE[*x,bc*]::=*if* atom [*x*] *then* print [*x*]; print ['']
                                                    else
                                   print [*bc*]; print ['('];
                                   MU[car [*x*],cdr[*x*]];
                                   print [')']; print [*bc*]; print ['']
                                   fi.

We see here several statements separated by semicolons, i.e. statements to be executed in sequence. Thus we define the following functions with dummy variables:

```
(PSP(LAMBDA(D)(PRIN1 BLANK)))
(PR(LAMBDA(D)(PRIN1 R)))
(PRNUM(LAMBDA(D)(PRIN1 BC)))
(PLPAR(LAMBDA(D)(PRIN1 LPAR)))
(PRPAR(LAMBDA(D)(PRIN1 RPAR)))
(MUX(LAMBDA(D)(MU(CAR X)(CDR X))))
```

The part of MU[*l,r*] above which starts with '*if*' must also be expressed as a function with a dummy variable, thus

```
0  1     2 22
(IF(LAMBDA(D)(COND
  34      4  3
  ((NULL R)NIL)
  34        44   5  6             6543
  ((ATOM R)(PSP(PR(PRIN1 PERIOD)))))
  3   4  5     543
  (T (MU(CAR R))))
210
)))
```

The function MU consists of two successive commands:

```
(MU(LAMBDA(L R)(IF(ANALYSE L(ADD1 BC)))))
```

and similarly for the function ANALYSE we get

```
0           1      2    22
(ANALYSE(LAMBDA(X BC)(COND
  34      44   5     543
  ((ATOM X)(PSP(PRIN1 X)))
  3  4   5     6      7    8     9         9876543
  (T(PSP(PRNUM(PRPAR(MUX(PLPAR(PRNUM T)))))))))
210
)))
```

Notice the form (PRNUM T) in ANALYSE. The parameter T is only there to satisfy the syntax, since PRNUM is a function of one (dummy) variable. T could be replaced by NIL or anything else which has a value. This form could have been replaced by (PRIN1 BC). Notice also that the last thing ANALYSE does is to execute the function PSP, the yield of which is the yield of the form BLANK, which is a space. This is therefore the yield of ANALYSE in all cases.

If we look at the definition of IF we notice that it contains the variable R which is not one of its formal parameters. It is in fact the formal parameter R of the function MU. We express this by saying that R 'occurs free' in the λ-expression for IF. This variable will automatically be given a value when IF is called by MU. We must think of IF as a function 'known' only to MU and we must not use IF in any other way. Further, MU contains the parameter BC free. Thus MU must also be 'hidden' from the user; it may only be used by ANALYSE. The Lisp system has no means of knowing these connections and therefore cannot issue meaningful error messages if such functions are misused. The user must therefore ensure that he/she uses only those functions defined in a program which are meant to be used. In the present example one is only supposed to use ANALYSE.

To see how to use it for practical purposes we must look at input and output.

3.3 Input and output

There are two standard functions for printing: PRIN1 and PRINT. The form (PRIN1 X) yields the value of X and prints this value, provided that it is an atom. The form (PRINT X) yields the value of X, which can be any S-expression, and prints it and then positions the printing device at the beginning of a new line. I will assume that there is also a function WRITE which is similar to PRINT but which does not automatically move to a new line. This function is not standard but something analogous is probably available in most Lisp systems.

READ is the function for reading data; it is a function of no variable. The form (READ) is evaluated as follows: the reading device is moved over the next S-expression at the top level and this expression is the yield of the form. Thus if we already have the bracket-counting function ANALYSE of the previous section we can write the following program {with computer responses preceded by '→'}:

```
(LAMBDA()(ANALYSE(READ)0)))()
  ((A(B.C)))
→ 0(1(A2(B.C)21)0
→{space, which is the yield of ANALYSE}
ANALYSE((P(Q R)) 1)
→ 1(P2(Q R)2)1
→{space}
```

We see here the only exception to the general rule that a program consists of pairs of S-expressions. Each pair may be followed by S-expressions which are data for READ. Whether more than one such S-expression datum may be written on the same line depends on the particular implementation. The same remark applies also to the usual pairs. For definiteness I assume that only one datum or one pair may appear on one line; of course an S-expression may occupy as many lines as desired since the end of the line is regarded simply as a space for these purposes. In practice one usually wants data, as well as programs to be read from files. There is no standard way of doing this so I will describe a simple method used by the Lisp/66 system, written by the University of Waterloo for the Honeywell 6000 series computers. There is a function OPENR of two variables. The call OPENR(2 INFILE) associates the number 2 with the existing file called INFILE. Thereafter the call RDS(2) will position the reading device at the beginning of that file. The contents of the file may be any Lisp program, i.e. pairs of S-expressions and possibly data for READ, as usual. When the end of the file is reached the reading device returns automatically to the standard device, e.g. the computer terminal which one is using.

For example, suppose the file FILE1 consists of a single S-expression in which we want to count the brackets. After

```
OPENR(3 FILE1)
```

we might be tempted to write

```
RDS(3)                                           {1}
(LAMBDA()(ANALYSE(READ)0))()                     {2}
```

but this will not work because after {1} the computer will read in FILE1 and so will not 'see' {2}. We must incorporate {1} and {2} into a single function call, e.g.

```
DEFINE((
  (FAN(LAMBDA(D)(ANALYSE(READ)0)))
  ))
```

and then

```
(LAMBDA()(FAN(RDS 3))))().
```

Here we have used the dummy variable D as explained previously. We could achieve the same effect by taking advantage of the fact that the yield of RDS is NIL when the call is made from the terminal, and write

```
OR((RDS 3)(ANALYSE(READ)O))
```

Here we have an example of an F-function used at the top level. If the yield of (RDS 3) is not NIL {which can happen} we would have to replace OR by AND. Because of these complications I usually avoid using AND and OR for such a purpose.

In general, a file will consist of many S-expressions and we shall want to bracket-count them all. One not very elegant way is to change the file by putting a '(' at the beginning and a ')' at the end, thus making it into a single list and then using the above method.

It is also probable that we shall run out of computer space because of the large size of the expression to be analysed. We can arrive at a better way as follows:

Every file is automatically terminated by an 'end of file' character which is never printed but is detected by READ. In this Lisp system the atom \$EOF\$ is provided. It has an APVAL equal to the 'end of file' character. This enables us to write something like

$$\left. \begin{array}{l} \text{FILECHECK::}=y\text{:=READ;} \\ \quad \textit{if } y = \text{\$EOF\$ } \textit{then } \text{'DONE'} \\ \quad \textit{else } \text{ANALYSE}[y,o]\text{;FILECHECK} \\ \quad \textit{fi} \end{array} \right\} \text{IF}[y]$$

This leads to

```
 0   1        2 22
(IF1(LAMBDA(Y)(COND
     34          44           43
    ((EQ Y $EOF$)(QUOTE DONE))
     3  4  5     55          6              6543
    (T(OR(TERPRI)(FILECHECK(ANALYSE Y O)))))
     210
    )))
(FILECHECK(LAMBDA(D)(IF1(READ)))))
```

Notice that OR is used in IF1 only in order to print each expression on a new line. Now to bracket-count the file NEW we write

```
OPENR(4 NEW)
(LAMBDA()(FILECHECK(RDS 4)))()
```

or, even more conveniently we could, in the bracket-counting program, define a function

```
(FILECOUNT(LAMBDA(N)(FILECHECK(RDS N))))
```

so we can simply call

```
(FILECOUNT(4).
```

{cf. Fig. 2 for an example}. If the system is such that READ will notice only one S-expression per line then some editing must be done, e.g. replace

```
DEFINE((
```

by

```
DEFINE
   ((
```

In this Lisp system there are similar methods for directing all computer printing to a file, which is often useful; the details are given in Section 5.2.

Chapter 4

Functions as Arguments

4.1 Functions as actual parameters

Just as in many other computer languages, procedures or functions can have formal parameters of type {or mode} function {or procedure} in Lisp.

Suppose U = U[s,ff] is the function which applies the function ff of two variables to the non-atomic S-expression s and yields the value of ff[car[s],cdr[s]]. This can be defined by

```
(U(LAMBDA(S FF)(FF(CAR S)(CDR S))))
```

If we now call

```
U((A B C)CONS)
```

we get (A B C)
and from

```
U(((A B)C D)APPEND)
```

we get (A B C D). Here the call on U is at the top level. If U appears at an inside level. i.e. in a form, then the actual function argument must be of type

```
(FUNCTION fn)
```

where fn is the actual function in question, e.g.

```
(LAMBDA(X)(U X(FUNCTION CONS)))((A B C))
```

The same rule holds quite generally. This rule does not apply if fn is to be evaluated first as in

$$\overset{0}{(}\text{LAMBDA}\overset{1}{(}\text{X FN}\overset{1}{)}\overset{1}{(}\text{CADR}\overset{2}{(}\text{U X FN}\overset{210012}{)))}\overset{2}{(}\overset{1}{(}\text{(A B}\overset{1}{)}\text{C D}\overset{0}{)}\text{APPEND}\overset{0}{)}$$

Here we do not write (FUNCTION FN) in the form (U X FN) since FN has to be evaluated first {yielding APPEND}.

A standard function with a formal parameter of type 'function' is MAPLIST. If *fn* is a function of one variable and *x* is the list $(a_1 a_2 - a_n)$ then

> MAPLIST$[x,fn]$

yields the list $(fn[(a_1-a_n)]fn[(a_2-a_n)]-fn[(a_n)])$. More often we use the less general function MAPCAR. With the above notation

> MAPCAR$[x,fn]$

yields the list $(fn[a_1]\ fn[a_2]-fn[a_n])$.

MAPCAR can be defined in terms of MAPLIST:

```
 0         1          2   2 2
(MAPCAR(LAMBDA(X  G)(MAPLIST X
      3      4          5 55  6        6543210
      (FUNCTION(LAMBDA(L)(G(CAR L))))))))
```

A certain amount of evaluation of the function parameter $\overset{4}{(}$LAMBDA $\overset{5}{(}$L$\overset{55}{)}$($\overset{6}{}$G$\overset{654}{(}$CAR L$)))$ must of course take place, viz. G needs to be evaluated but FUNCTION takes care of that.

4.2 EVAL

EVAL is a function of two variables. The second parameter is nearly always NIL so that in many Lisp systems EVAL is in fact a function of only one variable. If 'form' stands for a form which can be evaluated then a call EVAL [form,NIL] yields the value of that form. For instance, after

> CSET(U%(RED APPLE))

the top level call

> EVAL(U% NIL)

yields (RED APPLE),

and

> EVAL((CADR U%)NIL)

yields APPLE

If U% had not first been CSET an error would have resulted since the form (CADR U%) cannot be evaluated. If in this context we write, however,

> EVAL((CADR U%)((U% .(RED APPLE))))

the yield would again be APPLE. In this case the second parameter of EVAL is not NIL but a so-called ALIST {'association list'} which in general is a list of pairs of type

$$((x_1.a_1)(x_2.a_2)....)$$

where the x_i are atoms and the a_i S-expressions. If we denote this ALIST by 'alist' then

    EVAL[form,alist]

replaces any variables x_i which occur in the form by the corresponding a_i and then yields the value of the modified form. If several x_i in *alist* are equal it uses the left-most. The *alist* parameter if useful when we want to define special F-functions called FEXPRs, to be discussed later.

Note that EVAL is an ordinary function, not an F-function. After

```
CSET(A% B%)
CSET(B% JOHN)
(LAMBDA(X)(EVAL X NIL))(A%)
```

the yield is B%, and

```
(LAMBDA(X)(EVAL X NIL))(B%)
```

yields JOHN, and

```
(LAMBDA( )(EVAL A% NIL))( )
```

yields JOHN, and

```
(LAMBDA( )(EVAL(QUOTE A%)NIL))( )
```

yields B%.

Note that we could get B% from A% without EVAL, e.g. by

```
(LAMBDA( )A%)( )
```

which yields B%, but we cannot get JOHN from A% without EVAL. This function is therefore useful in accessing values indirectly.

4.3 Playing noughts and crosses (tic-tac-toe)

Let us set ourselves the task of writing a Lisp program for playing this simple game, the person {P} playing against the machine {M}. Although there is a simple strategy for playing the game correctly, we shall not use it as it is more interesting from the point of view of computing to let the machine discover the correct moves by simply following the consequences of every move it could make. A good way of writing fairly complicated programs is to write a skeleton outline {or blueprint} first, postponing various details to a later phase. In this way we discover the inner logic and find suitable ways of representing its various aspects to the machine. Names in braces, e.g. {OTHERWISE} indicate functions which will be defined, to help deal with what follows:

The main idea here is to give a *value* to each possible position in this game. The possible values are

```
MWIN,DRAW,PWIN
```

where, for example, MWIN means that when a player is confronted by this position it must result in a win for the machine with best play on both sides. This evaluation is done by the function EVALUATE; at the same time this function yields the best reply if the player is the machine. The following is an outline {or blueprint} for it:

EVALUATE[position,player]::=
{The player is confronted by the position}
{Q1}
Test whether the position is terminal {i.e. no legal reply is possible};
{POSSIBLE-REPL}
if yes then evaluate it by inspection and yield the value MWIN, DRAW or PWIN as the case may be {and EXIT};
{MAKEREPLIES}
if no, let L = list of all positions which result from the player making one legal move {there are as many of these as there are vacant squares}.
{IMMEDIATE-WIN}
Examine each position in L for a winning line. If one is found then yield MWIN or PWIN {according to whether the player is M or P}, together with the corresponding position if the player is M. If there is no such immediate win then examine again
{OTHERWISE}
each position M1 in L in the following way:
{WHL1}
let M2 = EVALUATE[M1,OTHER PLAYER];
{D01[M_1,M_2]}
let y = VALUE-OF M_2
{IF1[y]}
if player = M then

if y = MWIN then yield the value y and the position M1 {and EXIT}

else if y = DRAW then remember that M1 is a draw unless a draw has already been remembered among the positions in L

fi;

examine the next position in L {if there is one}

fi

else {player = P} proceed as above with MWIN replaced by PWIN but yield only the value y, not the position M1

fi;

{IF2}

{player has no winning move}

if a DRAW was remembered then yield the remembered item

else yield LOSS[PLAYER]

fi {end of EVALUATE}.

We can already convert this into a Lisp program with certain details replaced by question marks and comments. These will be filled in when we have decided how to represent positions. We can now write:

```
0         1    2 (POS  PLAYER)
(EVALUATE(LAMBDA(POS  PLAYER)

  2  3                    3210
  (Q1(POSSIBLE-REPL POS PLAYER))))
 0  1      2 22     3
 (Q1(LAMBDA(L)(COND({L is a reply to a terminal position}
                                                        3
                            {yield MWIN or DRAW or PWIN})
     3 4        5              543
     (T(OTHERWISE(IMMEDIATE-WIN L PLAYER)))
 210
 )))
```

We can decide now that IMMEDIATE-WIN yields NIL if there is no immediate win. Using this we write

```
  0         1       2 22   3   3
  (OTHERWISE(LAMBDA(X)(COND(X X)
   3 4        43210
   (T(WHL1 ? ?)))))))
```

Thus otherwise [x] yields x if x is not NIL.

We shall make WHL1 a function of two variables, REMEMBER and L2. The purpose of REMEMBER is to 'remember' a draw and L2 is the list of possible replies not yet examined. When WHL1 is called first then REMEMBER has value NIL and L2 has value L, the list of all

possible replies {eight at most}. Thus '? ?' in OTHERWISE is to be
replaced by NIL L and WHL1 is defined as:

```
 0      1       2          2 2
(WHL1(LAMBDA(REMEMBER L2)(COND
  3 4       4 4         4 3
  ((NULL L2)(IF2 REMEMBER))
  3 4   5       5 5       6      6
  (T(DO1(CAR L2)(EVALUATE(CAR L2)
     6            6
     (OTHER PLAYER)
  5 4 3
  )))
2 1 0
)))
```

The function IF2 yields the remembered information if there was a
draw, otherwise it yields LOSS[PLAYER]:

```
 0    1        2  2 2     3    3 3  3              4 3 2 1 0
(IF2(LAMBDA(R((COND(R R)(T(LOSS PLAYER)))))
 0    1       1          2 2
(LOSS)LAMBDA(PLAYER)(COND
  3 4     5            5 5          5 4 3
  ((EQ PLAYER(QUOTE M)(QUOTE PWIN)))
  3 4         4 3
  (T(QUOTE MWIN))
2 1 0
)))
(DO1(LAMBDA(M1 M2)(IF1(VALUE-OF M2)))).
```

At this point it becomes desirable to consider the details of the
representation of positions and their values.

I chose the following obvious representation: the nine squares are
numbered 1,2–9 and the initial situation is represented by the list (1 2 3 4
5 6 7 8 9). The position

is represented by the list (1(2.P)3 4 5(6.M)(7.P)8 9) and so on. The only
disadvantage of this representation is that it is not easy to detect a
terminal position such as ((1.P)(2.P)(3.M)4(5.M)6(7.P)8(9.P)). No
doubt better representations exist; in any case all the above functions
are valid for all representations.

It is quite easy for PLAYER to 'take' square N. Let us suppose that
BOARD% has been CSET to a position. Then

```
 0        1      2          2 2
(TAKE(LAMBDA((N PLAYER)(MAPCAR BOARD%
     3        4       5  5 5
     (FUNCTION(LAMBDA(S)(COND
        6 7        7 7         7 6 6    6
        ((EQUAL N S)(CONS S PLAYER ))(T S)
     5 4 3
     )))
 2 1 0
 )))
```

does this in an elegant way. Note that BOARD% is not changed by this function.

The function IF1 must in certain cases yield both a reply {i.e. a position} and its value. An obvious way of representing such a pair is in the form

```
(VALUE.POSITION).
```

Using this we can write

```
DEFINE(((VALUE-OF CAR)))
```

{VALUE-OF is 'called' in DO1}. Let us suppose that we have the function WIN such that WIN[POS,PLAYER] yields *T* if the position POS contains a won 'line' for PLAYER, otherwise it yields NIL, e.g. if the position (1.P)(2.P)(3.P)(4.M)(5.M) 6 (7.M) 8 9) is *pos* then WIN[*pos*,P] yields *T*. If *ll* is a list of positions {such as we get from POSSIBL-REPL} then IMMEDIATE-WIN[*ll*,M] yields (MWIN.POS) where POS is the first member of *ll* which contains a won 'line' for M; if there is no such position the yield is NIL. IMMEDIATE-WIN[*ll*,P] is similar but instead of yielding (PWIN.POS) it simply yields (PWIN). Why does it yield (PWIN) rather than the atom PWIN? That is because we have decided that VALUE-OF is CAR in all cases.

Let H1 [*pos*,*player*] have the yield just described {in the case where *pos* contains a winning line}. Thus

```
 0  1      2          2 2
(H1(LAMBDA(POS PLAYER)(COND
    3 4       5        5 4
    ((EQ PLAYER(QUOTE M))
      4     5         5  4 3
      (CONS(QUOTE MWIN)POS))
    3 4     5       5 4 3
    (T(QUOTE(PWIN))))
 2 1 0
 )))
```

and then

```
 0                 1         2       2 2
(IMMEDIATE-WIN(LAMBDA(LL  PLAYER)(COND
   3 4      4  3
  ((NULL  LL)NIL)
   3 4    5          4 4   5    5      4 3
  ((WIN(CAR  LL)PLAYER)(H1(CAR  LL)PLAYER))
   3 4              5         4 3
  (T(IMMEDIATE-WIN(CDR  LL)PLAYER))
 2 1 0
)))
```

We can now continue writing down functions using the blueprint:

```
 0   1        2  2 2
(IF1(LAMBDA(Y)(COND
   3 4     5           5 4
  ((EQ  PLAYER(QUOTE  M))
     4
    (COND
       5 6    7       7 6
      ((EQ  Y(QUOTE  MWIN))
         6        6 5
        (CONS  Y  M1))
       5 6    7     8         8 7
      ((AND(EQ  Y(QUOTE  DRAW))
          7                7
         (NULL  REMEMBER)
         6
        )
         6     7          7 7       7 6 5
        (WHL1(CONS  Y  M1)(CDR  L2)))
       5 6                7        7 6 5
      (T(WHL1  REMEMBER(CDR  L2)))
     4 3
    ))
   3 4   5             5 4 4    5      5 4 3
  ((EQ  Y(QUOTE  PWIN))(QUOTE(PWIN)))
   3 4   5      6          6 5 5             5 4
  ((AND(EQ  Y(QUOTE  DRAW))(NULL  REMEMBER))
     4      5        5 5        5 4
    (WHL  1(LIST  Y)(CDR  L2))
     3
    )
   3 4           5          5 4 3
  (T(WHL1  REMEMBER(CDR  L2)))
 2 1 0
)))
```

We now turn to POSSIBLE-REPL. Informally we write

```
POSSIBLE-REPL[pos,player]::=
    IF WIN[pos,OTHER[player]]THEN yield LOSS[player]
{BLA} ELSE let ll = MAKEREPLIES[pos,player];
```

```
IF ll ≠ NIL THEN yield(ll)
ELSE yield (DRAW)
FI
```

which gives

```
 0            1     2          2
(POSSIBLE-REPL(LAMBDA(POS PLAYER)
 2
 (COND
  34        5          544          43
  ((WIN POS(OTHER PLAYER))(LOSS PLAYER))
  3 4   5                   543
  (T(BLA(MAKEREPLIES POS PLAYER)))
  210
  )))
 (BLA(LAMBDA(LL)(COND(LL LL)(T(QUOTE(DRAW)))))))
```

MAKEREPLIES[*pos,player*] makes a list of all positions which are immediate possible replies that the *player* can make when confronted by the position *pos*. If there are no vacant squares then it yields NIL. To write this function is a good exercise which the reader might like to try before looking at the following solution.

Informally, Let w = MAKEREPLIES[CDR[*pos*],player];{if *pos* ≠ NIL} stick on CAR[*pos*] in front of each position in w; let STICK be the resulting list; let x be the position obtained from *pos* by 'occupying' its first square if it is not already occupied in which case yield CONS[x, STICK], otherwise yield STICK. Take STICK as a function of no variables:

```
 0     1      222     3          4            43
(STICK(LAMBDA()(MAPCAR(MAKEREPLIES(CDR POS PLAYER))
      3        4     5 55   6        6 543210
      (FUNCTION(LAMBDA(X)(CONS(CAR POS)X))))))
```

and then

```
 0           1     2          2
(MAKEREPLIES(LAMBDA(POS PLAYER)
 2     34         4    3
 (COND((NULL POS)NIL)
       34     5    5  54
       ((ATOM(CAR (POS))          {the square is unoccupied}
         4
         (CONS
          5
          (CONS
           6    7         7      6
           (CONS(CAR POS)PLAYER)
           6       6
           (CDR POS)
```

```
     5
     )
     5        5
     (STICK)
   43
   ))
  3 4      43
  (T(STICK))
 210
 )))
```

We now fill in the missing items in the function Q1, the case where the position POS in EVALUATE is terminal. In that case POSSIBLE-REPL will have yielded (MWIN), (PWIN) or (DRAW) and these we want to be also the yield of Q1. The missing items are the pair of S-expressions

```
 4
 (OR
  5        6      7      765
  (EQUAL  L(QUOTE(MWIN)))
  5        6      7      765
  (EQUAL  L(QUOTE(PWIN)))
  5        6      7      765
  (EQUAL  L(QUOTE(DRAW)))
 4
 )
```

and L.

We now turn to the function WIN, discussed earlier. It is useful here to use the standard function MEMBER. MEMBER[u,v] is *T* if the S-expression u is a member of the list v, NIL otherwise. We shall use it in the related function SUBSET, another predicate, SUBSET[a,b] is *T* if and only if every member of the list a is also a member of the list b (i.e. $a \subset b$)

```
 0       1        2        2 2   3        3
 (SUBSET(LAMBDA(A B)(OR(NULL A)
  3    4       5       5 4
  (AND(MEMBER(CAR A)B)
   4       5       5 4
   (SUBSET(CDR A)B)
  3
  )
 210
 )))
```

Let us CSET MWIN% to the list of eight elements

```
 012    22     22    21
 (((1.M)(2.M)(3.M))
  12    22     22    21
  ((4.M)(5.M)(6.M))
  etc.
  12    22     22    210
  ((7.M)(5.M)(3.M)))
```

which are all the possible winning lines for the machine and let PWIN% be similarly CSET to all possible winning lines for the player P. Checking whether position *pos* contains a winning line for player M is equivalent to verifying that an element of MWIN% is a SUBSET of *pos*. This can be done by the function LOOP1:

```
 0       1        2      22     34       4   3
(LOOP1(LAMBDA(L POS)(COND((NULL L)NIL)
   34      5      5    4 3
  ((SUBSET(CAR L)POS)T)
   3 4      5      5   4 3
  (T(LOOP1(CDR L)POS))
 210
)))
```

and then

```
(WIN(LAMBDA(POS PLAYER)(COND
  ((EQ PLAYER(QUOTE M))
    (LOOP1 MWIN% POS))
  (T(LOOP1 PWIN% POS))
)))
```

All functions mentioned so far are now completely defined. The rest is concerned with convenient input and output. First we define

```
 0      1        222        3
(START(LAMBDA()(CSETQ BOARD%(QUOTE
   4
  (1 2 3 4 5 6 7 8 9)
 3210
))))
```

and next a function which changes BOARD%

```
(PUTS(LAMBDA(N PLAYER)(CSETQ BOARD%
  (TAKE N PLAYER)
)))
```

and now the function IGO such that IGO[*n*] puts the P in square *n*, modifies BOARD% accordingly, then calls EVALUATE [BOARD%,M], then CSETs BOARD% to the resulting position {throwing away its value} and finally prints BOARD%:

```
 0     1      2 22
(IGO(LAMBDA(N)(AND
   3    4      43
  (PUTS N(QUOTE P))
   3    4            5        543
  (CSETQ BB%(EVALUATE BOARD%(QUOTE M)))
   3          4      43
  (CSETQ BOARD%(CDR BB%))
```

```
     3                  3
    (PRINT BOARD%)
  210
   )))
```

BB% is used for clarity; one could use BOARD% instead. BOARD%
is being used here in the way in which assignments are made to variables
in conventional programming languages.

To play the game we type

```
    START(  )
```

and then, if the person is to play first,

```
    IGO(3)
```

if the person wants to occupy square 3. The machine will print out the
board with its reply already in place and so on. This process can be
repeated as often as desired. It is probable that the machine will run out
of space or time when trying to make its first move since it has to
examine an enormous number of positions. It is better to let the
machine start first by using PUTS (n M) before IGO at the start of the
game. Note that the machine makes no reply if every reply is a losing
one. What the computer prints here is not very legible; the following
paragraph shows how to improve it.

4.4 Layout

We can easily define various layout routines and formats. I find the
following useful, an idea that occurs in Algol 68 and elsewhere. Suppose
that format is any list, say $(h_1 \; h_2 – h_m)$, the h_i being any S-expression. To
print the list $(a_1 – a_n)$ using the format means printing a_1 using h_1, a_2 using
h_2 etc. where, if $n > m$, the format starts again from the beginning
whenever it has been 'exhausted'. What is meant by printing a according
to h depends on what the user requires. Consider the simple case where
it is to mean: first print a without taking a new line; then if h is NIL take
a new line. To achieve this I shall define a function OUTF such that
OUTF[l,*format*] prints the list l using the *format*. As is often the case,
we need to generalize the problem before we can solve it. Suppose that
after printing some of the elements of l using the format $f1$ we are left
with the list $l2$ of elements of l not yet printed, and the corresponding
unused part of $f2$ of $f1$. This situation is to be dealt with by the function
call OUTF2[$l2, f1, f2$] in terms of which

```
    OUTF(LAMBDA(L FORMAT)(OUTF2 L FORMAT FORMAT))
```

Assuming that USING is a function of one dummy variable which specifies what is to be done after printing *a* (using *f*) we have

```
 0     1       2       22   34        4       3
(OUTF2(LAMBDA(L2 F1 F2)(COND((NULL L2)BLANK)
  34      44        43
 ((NULL F2)(OUTF L2 F1))
  3 4    5       6     6543
 (T(USING(WRITE(CAR L2))))
 210
))))
```

Here USING::=

```
    if CAR[F2]≠NIL then NIL else TERPRI[]fi;
{SS}  OUTF2[CDR[L2],F1,CDR[F2]]
```

which can be writen, using dummy variables:

```
 0     1      2 22 3      45      5   4
(USING(LAMBDA(D)(SS(COND((CAR F2)NIL)
  4 5     54
 (T(TERPRI))
 3210
))))
(SS(LAMBDA(D)(OUTF2(CDR L2)F1(CDR F2)))).
```

We can use OUTF to improve the layout in the noughts and crosses program of Section 4.3. To do this we change the last line of the function IGO.

We introduce the function LAYOUT:

```
(LAYOUT(LAMBDA(X)(COND((ATOM X)X)
  (T(CDR X)))))
```

which is used for printing information about the square X; if X is occupied it is of the form (*n*.M) or (*n*.P) in which case we want to print only M or P; if it is unoccupied we want its number. Next we do

```
CSET(FORMAT%(A A NIL))
```

The last line of IGO is changed to

```
(OUTF(MAPCAR BOARD%(FUNCTION LAYOUT))FORMAT%)          {†}
```

† See Chapter 5 for a discussion on using MAPCAR in this way.

This will print positions in the form

```
1MP
45M
PM9
```

with no spaces between the symbols

    A more powerful facility is to take format as a list of type (h_1-h_n) where the h_i, are functions of no argument. In this case, 'print *a* using *h*' means; print *a* and then call $h[\ ]$. To achieve this, all we need to do is to change the definitions of USING to

```
 0       1          2  22  3      4       5        5 4      3 2 1 0
(USING(LAMBDA(D)(SS(EVAL(LIST(CAR F2))NIL)))).
```

With this we can introduce a space after each square printed in the noughts and crosses program by

```
CSET(FORMAT%(SPACE SPACE TERPRI))
```

where

```
(SPACE(LAMBDA()(PRIN1 BLANK)))
```

instead of the previous format. The reader should make sure he/she understands why LIST and EVAL are used in the body of USING.

Chapter 5

Trees

5.1 Trees and forests

A lot of computing is concerned with 'trees' and Lisp is particularly good for this purpose. The concept 'tree' and 'forest' is defined by a 'mutually recursive' definition such as the following {in BNF notation}

```
<forest>::=<tree>|<forest><tree>|empty.
<tree>::=<root><forest>.
<root>::=<node>.
```

A <node> can be any one of a class of objects which one wishes to manipulate. In Chapter 4, for instance, there was an implicit tree whose nodes were the various positions which were to be examined. The terminal positions were trees which consist only of the root. If we call the <forest> in the definition of <tree> the progeny {or sons} of its root then a 'terminal node' is a tree, the progeny of whose root is the empty forest. Such nodes are, for obvious reasons, also called 'leaves'. We shall not go into the further theory of trees but will turn to a concrete example.

The game tree of the noughts and crosses game was never visible since it was 'grown' by the program. Another situation arises if one is given a large amount of 'data' which one wishes to arrange into a tree in order to be able to manipulate the data in a relatively simple way. This arises in the following type of problem.

5.2 A tape recorder index

I have a tape recorder and several reels of tape. Each tape has two sides and on each side the tape recorder can record and play back from one or other of two 'tracks'. When a tape is played or is recording, a revolution counter counts the amount of tape that has passed through the machine. Thus any item recorded can be identified by the following data: tape number; the side (1 or 2); the track (1 or 2); the counter number at the start; the counter number at the end; and details of the item.

I wished to make an index of all items already recorded and to write a program which would enable me to add new items and delete old ones from the index. I should want an index printed in such a way that items should be listed in the order in which they appear on a track of a tape.

I decided, for reasons which will become clear, to represent an item as the following S-expression

```
(tape-number(side(track(starting-counter-number(TO
(finish-counter-number and details)))))).
```

An example of an item is

```
(3(2(1(340(TO 550 MOZART * STRING QUARTET K428))))).
```

Such an item, which I call a piece, I regard as a special kind of tree, usually called a 'branch'. It can be depicted thus:

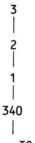

```
            TO 550 MOZART * STRING QUARTET K428
```

Its root is 3 and its progeny is again a branch, etc. The item starting with 'TO 550' is its only leaf. All pieces on tape 3 will be made into a tree whose root is 3. For instance, the piece

```
(3(2(2(1(TO 161 HAYDN * STRING QUARTET OP64 NO4))))))
```

together with the previous pieces makes the tree

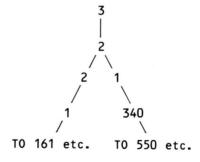

The trees representing all the tapes constitute a forest which I call the index. There are of course many suitable ways of representing trees and forests as S-expressions. I choose here the simple representation suggested by the definition given earlier: the forest consisting of the trees t_1,t_2-t_k in that order is represented by the list $(t_1\ t_2-t_k)$ so that the empty forest is NIL. The tree with root r and progeny p (which is a forest) is represented by $(r.p)$. Thus the tree with root r and progeny $(t_1\ t_2)$ is $(r\ t_1\ t_2)$. We can therefore at once define the functions ROOT and PROGENY:

```
DEFINE((
  (ROOT CAR)(PROGENY CDR)
))
```

The ordering of the trees in a forest is to be here in descending order of their roots {the roots being numbers}. It is a feature of most programming on trees that functions occur in pairs, the functions in each pair calling on each other {mutual recursion}. One of the functions of the pair deals with forests, the other with trees. For instance, we want to insert a piece in the index. This is done by the function MERGE. This function calls on INSERT which inserts the piece in a tree which has the same root number as the piece. MERGE finds such a tree in the forest, if there is one, otherwise it puts the piece {regarded as a tree} into its proper place in the forest.

```
 0         1     2           2 2   3        3
(INSERT(LAMBDA(PIECE TREE)(CONS(ROOT TREE)
  3     4         4
  (MERGE(CADR PIECE)
    4          4
    (PROGENY TREE)
  3
  )
2 1 0
)))


 0        1     2           2
(MERGE(LAMBDA(PIECE FOREST)
  2     3 4          4 4          4 3
  (COND((NULL FOREST)(CONS PIECE NIL))
    3 4      5             5 5   6        6 5 4
    ((EQUAL(ROOT PIECE)(ROOT(CAR FOREST)))
      4     5             6          6 5
      (CONS(INSERT PIECE(CAR FOREST))
        5         5
        (CDR FOREST)
      4
      )
```

```
 3
 )
 3 4        5               5 5   6              6 5 4
((GREATERP(ROOT PIECE)(ROOT(CAR FOREST)))
   4              4
   (CONS PIECE FOREST)
 3
 )
 3 4    5            5 5         6           6 5 4 3
(T(CONS(CAR FOREST)(MERGE PIECE(CDR FOREST))))
 2
 )
10
))
```

We need a similar pair of functions to remove a piece, FREMOVE
and TREMOVE:

```
 0        1      2              2 2   3          3
(TREMOVE(LAMBDA(PIECE TREE)(CONS(ROOT PIECE)
 3
 (FREMOVE
   4    5              5 4 4           4
   (CAR(PROGENY PIECE))(PROGENY TREE)
 3
 )
2 1 0
)))
```

It is assumed that the TREE in TREMOVE is not a piece.

```
 0        1      2                2 2
(FREMOVE(LAMBDA(PIECE FOREST)(COND
 3 4         4   3
((NULL FOREST)NIL)
 3 4    5         5 5   6              6 5 4
((EQUAL(ROOT PIECE)(ROOT(CAR FOREST)))
   4     5 6      7              7 6 6         6 5
   (COND((ISPIECE(CAR FOREST))(CDR FOREST))
     5 6    7              8           8 7
     (T(CONS(TREMOVE PIECE(CAR FOREST))
       7        7 6
       (CDR FOREST))
     5
     )
   4
   )
 3
 )
 3 4    5            5 5              6           6 5 4 3
(T(CONS(CAR FOREST)(FREMOVE PIECE(CDR FOREST))))
2 1 0
)))
```

The predicate ISPIECE [*tree*] tests whether *tree* is a piece, i.e. a branch:
it yields *T* if either *tree* is terminal {tested by ISTERMINAL} or if the

progeny of *tree* is a forest whose only member is a piece.

```
 0       1       2    22 3                   3
(ISPIECE(LAMBDA(TREE)(OR(ISTERMINAL TREE)
    3   4    5    6              654
   (AND(NULL(CDR(PROGENY TREE)))
       4      5    6              654
      (ISPIECE(CAR(PROGENY TREE)))
    3
    )
 210
 )))
(ISTERMINAL(LAMBDA(TREE)(EQ(ROOT TREE)(QUOTE TO))))
```

We now have all the functions needed for inserting and removing pieces in the index. We still need functions for printing the index in a legible fashion.

For convenience I define a function WRITEOUT which prints an S-expression and follows it by two blanks:

```
(WRITEOUT(LAMBDA(X)(AND(WRITE X)(PRIN1 BLANK)
                                (PRIN1 BLANK)
 )))
```

PRINTPIECE prints a PIECE:

```
 0          1       2     22
(PRINTPIECE(LAMBDA(PIECE)(COND
    34               44         43
   ((ISTERMINAL PIECE)(PRINT PIECE))
    34       5            544       5   6
   ((WRITEOUT(ROOT PIECE))(PRINTPIECE(CAR(PROGENY
                                         6543
                                 PIECE))))
 210
 )))
```

Notice that the second pair in the above COND form, which starts with ((WRITEOUT, has a 'side-effect' of doing some printing. This is a useful way of shortening programs. It would not work if the yield of (WRITEOUT(ROOT PIECE)) were NIL so we must be careful when using this device. Note also the reason for having the CAR in (CAR (PROGENY PIECE)); a beginner might easily have omitted it. It is there because (PROGENY PIECE) is a forest {whose only member is the PIECE} and for PRINTPIECE we need a PIECE.

Next comes a function which prints a tree in such a way that each of its pieces starts on a new line.

```
 0            1      2    2 2
(PRINTTREE(LAMBDA(TREE)(COND
   3 4          4 4              4 3
   ((ISPIECE TREE)(PRINTPIECE TREE))
   3 4        5             5 4
   ((PRINTPIECE(FIRSTPIECE TREE))
    4          5          5 4 3
     (PRINTTREE(RESTOF TREE)))
 2 1 0
 )))
```

We are again using a COND pair with side-effects.

The functions FIRSTPIECE and RESTOF have the obvious meaning and are defined thus:

```
 0            1      2    2 2
(FIRSTPIECE(LAMBDA(TREE)(COND
   3 4          4   3
   ((ISPIECE TREE)TREE)
   3 4    5         5 5         6     7            7 6 5 4 3
   (T(LIST(ROOT TREE)(FIRSTPIECE(CAR(PROGENY TREE)))))))
 2 1 0
 )))
```

```
(RESTOF(LAMBDA(TREE)(TREMOVE(FIRSTPIECE TREE)TREE)))
```

Finally we print a whole forest by applying PRINTTREE to each of its members, from left to right.

```
 0             1      2      2 2
(PRINTFOREST(LAMBDA(FOREST)(MAPCAR FOREST
   3          4       5 5 5      6              6       5 4 3
   (FUNCTION(LAMBDA(X)(AND(PRINT TREE X)NIL)))
 2 1 0
 )))
```

The form (AND(PRINT TREE X)NIL) ensures that the yeilds of PRINT FOREST is as simple as possible, i.e. a list of type (NIL–NIL), one NIL for each tree in the forest, rather than some unwanted S-expression. It is assumed that MAPCAR$[x,f]$ applies the function f to the list x from left to right {cf. Section 5.3}.

I find it convenient to store the index on a disc file. I use the atom IND% to access the index. Initially when there was as yet nothing on the file I did

```
CSET(IND% NIL).
```

I prepared a file in which were written the various pieces {in any order} in the form explained in the beginning. Having opened the file {see Chapter 3} on channel 1, I wrote:

```
(LAMBDA()(MAKELOTS(RDS 1)))()
```

having first defined the following functions:

```
 0         1       2 22     3       3210
(MAKELOTS(LAMBDA(D)(AUXMAKE(READ)))))
 0        1      2 22
(AUXMAKE(LAMBDA(X)(COND
  34            44              43
  ((EQ X $EOF$)(QUOTE FINISHED))
  3 4          5         543
  (T(MAKELOTS(MAKEONE X)))
210
))))

(MAKEONE(LAMBDA(X)(CSETQ IND%(MERGE X IND%))))
```

The system provides a function OPENW which enables one to open a file on a channel number for writing, e.g.

```
OPENW(2 INDEX)
```

and a function WRS for writing to a file on a given channel number. I then wrote

```
OR((WRS 2)(PRINT IND%))
```

where advantage is taken of the fact that in this situation (WRS 2) yields NIL {otherwise I might have used AND instead of OR}. Note that the forms following OR are evaluated as required {unexpectedly!} because OR is an F-function.

The current index is now on the file INDEX in the form of a forest followed by the yield of OR {which is *T*}. This yield and any other items other than the valueof IND% {a single S-expression} must be removed before INDEX can be used again.

Suppose that subsequently I wish to remove a certain piece from the index and to add a new one. This can be done by the following:

```
CSET(P1%(4(1(1(210(TO BLA))))))
CSET(P2%(5(1(2(136(TO 240 BACH * PARTITA 0
                              GOTT(ORGAN)))))))
OPENR(1 INDEX)
OR((RDS 1)(CSETQ IND%(READ)))
EVAL((CSETQ IND%(FREMOVE P1% IND%))NIL)
EVAL((CSETQ IND%(MERGE P2% IND%))NIL)
EVAL((PRINTFOREST IND%)NIL)
OPENW(2 NEWINDEX)
OR((WRS 2)(PRINT IND%))
```

This gives me a printing of the updated index and the new index is also on the file NEWINDEX. Note that the piece P1% which is to be removed need have no details written after TO, as shown above.

5.3   On the order in which arguments are evaluated

In the *Lisp Manual* no explicit mention is made of the order in which the arguments of a function are evaluated but it is often assumed to be from left to right. It is nevertheless possible that a Lisp system evaluates them in another, possibly unspecified order, perhaps for the sake of efficiency and this may well become an important feature, as mentioned in the introduction. This order is usually unimportant but is crucial if the evaluation involves 'side-effects' such as printing, as was the case in the previous example. We can force any order of evaluation we like by using functions of only one variable. For instance, the usual function MAPCAR can be defined by

```
 0      1       2      22
(MAPCAR(LAMBDA(X  FN)(COND
   34      4   3
   ((NULL X)NIL)
   3 4    5   6    66   7      7   6543
   (T(CONS(FN(CAR X)(MAPCAR(CDR X)FN))))
 210
 )))
```

and then a call

```
MAPCAR((1 2 3 4 5)PRIN1)
```

will produce the side effect of printing

```
12345
```

provided that in evaluating the form

```
(CONS...)
```

the first argument is evaluated before the second. In the contrary case, 54321 would be printed. We can ensure that the function FN is applied from left to right to the list X by defining a function of one variable:

```
(NEWCONS(LAMBDA(Y)(CONS Y(MAPCAR(CDR X)FN))))
```

and replacing in MAPCAR the form (CONS. . .) by

```
(NEWCONS(FN(CAR X))).
```

This ensures that (FN(CAR X)) is evaluated before

    `(MAPCAR(CDR  X)FN).`

If we want application of FN from right to left we define

    `(CONS1(LAMBDA(Y)(CONS(FN(CAR  X))Y)))`

and change the form (CONS. . . .) in MAPCAR to

    `(CONS1(MAPCAR(CDR  X)FN))`

The same method can be used in all relevant cases.

Chapter 6

Property Lists

6.1 DEFLIST

DEFLIST is a function of two variables. The first variable stands for a list of pairs such as

$$((a_1 \ s_1)(a_1 \ s_2) - (a_k \ s_k))$$

where the a_i are atoms {non-numeric} and the s_i are arbitary S-expressions. The second variable stands for a non-numeric atom, called the 'indicator'. An example:

```
        0 1 2    3              3 2
DEFLIST(((JOHN(BORN  16  1  1980))

              2    3             3 2 1
              (MARY(BORN  20  3  1961)))
                   0
         BIRTHDAY)
```

Here the indicator is BIRTHDAY. .he yield of this call is the list (JOHN MARY) but the important thing is its side-effect. The effect is to associate with the atoms JOHN and MARY the indicator BIRTHDAY with the corresponding 'properties'

```
    (BORN  16  1  1980)
and (BORN  20  3  1961)
```

respectively. This association lasts until one does some explicit act to change it. We can now {or before} write

```
DEFLIST(((MARY(MOTHER OF JOHN)))RELATIVES)
```

and thus the atom MARY will now also have the indicator RELATIVES with property (MOTHER OF JOHN). We can associate as many indicators and corresponding properties with an atom as we wish. The totality of these indicators and properties are called the property list of the atom. The function GET has two variables, both being non-numeric atoms. The second stands for an indicator which might be on the atom represented by the first variable. The yield of GET[a b] is the property with indicator *b* associated with *a*, NIL if there is none. Thus after the above two calls

```
GET(JOHN BIRTHDAY)
```

yields

```
(BORN 16 1 1980)
```
and `GET(JOHN RELATIVES)`

yields NIL.
If we now write

```
DEFLIST((MARY(SISTER OF BOB))
        (JOHN(SON OF MARY)))RELATIVES)
```

then the new property associated with MARY with indicator RELA-TIVES is (SISTER OF BOB), the previous property (MOTHER OF JOHN) is now lost forever. If we wish to remove the BIRTHDAY and corresponding property from MARY we write

```
REMPROP(MARY BIRTHDAY).
```

If we wish to add further information to a property of an atom under a given indicator without erasing the property already there we can do it by defining the function

```
 0        1       2            2
(CHANGE(LAMBDA(A IND NEWENTRY)
   2        3    4      5             6
  (DEFLIST(LIST(LIST A(CONS NEWENTRY(GET
        6543    210
A IND))))IND))).
```

If we now write

```
CHANGE(JOHN RELATIVES(SON OF JACOB))
```
then `GET(JOHN RELATIVES)`

yields

```
((SON OF JACOB)SON OF MARY).
```

The function call

```
PRINTPROP(JOHN)
```

will print in some fashion all indicators and corresponding properties of JOHN. In some implementations this can also be achieved by the {illegal} call CDR(JOHN).

Some Lisp programmers are very fond of the property lists; I have not found them terribly useful; it probably depends on the sort of computation one wishes to do. Artificial intelligence programs use them quite often. One can get the same sort of effect by using CSET, e.g.

```
CSET(JOHN((BIRTHDAY(16 1 1980))
     (RELATIVES(SON OF JACOB)
       (SON OF MARY))
  ))
```

only one would then have to write functions corresponding to CHANGE and GET, which is easy.

6.2   FEXPRs

One of the main uses of DEFLIST is to write F-functions {mentioned in Chapter 3}. These are functions which cheat the normal Lisp semantics for the sake of convenience. Such a function is called a 'FEXPR'. A FEXPR can differ from a normal function in two ways: it can have any (undetermined) number of variables and when the FEXPR G, say, appears in a form

$$(G \ a_1 \ a_2-)$$

the parameters a_i are not evaluated unless the programmer specifically ensured that some {or all} are evaluated. A familiar example is CSETQ which is usually built in {in which case it is an FSUBR} but which we could define as an FEXPR. This function takes only two variables and only the second is evaluated. We could define it by

```
        0 1
DEFLIST((

           2        3        4   4 4     5      5 5
          (CSETQ(LAMBDA(X Y)(CSET(CAR X)(EVAL
            6   7    76 5432
            (CAR(CDR X))Y)))))
          1      0
          )FEXPR)
```

We must look at the way a form $(G \ a_1 \ a_2-)$ is treated by the Lisp system if G is an FEXPR or an FSUBR. First the unevaluated arguments are formed into a list arglist = $(a_1 \ a_2-)$. The FEXPR G will have been defined by

```
DEFLIST((

        (G(LAMBDA(X Y)-
        )FEXPR);
```

in all cases there will be exactly two formal parameters in the LAMBDA expression. The first parameter {X} will become 'bound' to arglist and the second parameter will become 'bound' to the current 'ALIST'. The ALIST is an internal 'stack' which contains all information regarding the 'bindings' of variables, i.e. it tells the system what values the variables stand for. The ALIST is in fact the second parameter of EVAL, about which we have so far said nothing. We only need to know that the form (EVAL z a) evaluates the S-expression z correctly if a evaluates to the current ALIST. In our previous examples there were no variables in z so we simply took the parameter a as NIL since its value was irrelevent. After this digression we return to the evaluation of (G a_1 a_2–). Let g stand for the LAMBDA expression used in the definition of G. Then the evaluation is precisely like the function call $g[(a_1\ a_2–),\ alist]$ {with *alist* replaced by the current ALIST}. For example, having defined the FEXPR CSETQ as above, the form

    (CSETQ B% W)

where W is a variable whose value is (BCD) will result in the call {if it were made at the top level}

$$
\begin{array}{l}
\overset{0}{(}\text{LAMBDA}\overset{1}{(}\text{X Y}\overset{1}{)}\overset{1}{(}\text{CSET}\overset{2}{(}\text{CAR X}\overset{2}{)}\overset{2}{(}\text{EVAL} \\
\overset{3}{(}\text{CAR}\overset{4}{(}\text{CDR X}\overset{4}{)}\overset{3}{)}\text{Y}\overset{2}{)}\overset{1}{)}\overset{0}{)}\ \overset{0}{(}\overset{1}{(}\text{B\% W}\overset{1}{)}alist\overset{0}{)}
\end{array}
$$

(CAR X) evaluates to B%, (CAR(CDR X)) evaluates to W and Y evaluates to *alist* {i.e. the current ALIST}. The form

    (EVAL(CAR(CDR X))Y)

evaluates EVAL[W,*alist*]
and since *alist* contains the information about W this evaluates to (BCD), so altogether we get the same as the call

    CSET[B%,(BCD)]

which is the effect we wanted.

As another example let us write OR as an FEXPR. A method for doing this in general, is to write a tentative function first, say ORF, which we modify later. ORF is supposed to be like OR but only takes one parameter which is thought of as being the list of parameters for

Chapter 6

OR. At this stage we don't worry about whether things get evaluated or not.

```
ORF[l]::=.
            if l=NIL then NIL
            else if car[l]=NIL then orf[cdr[l]]
            else *T*.
```

Now we modify it so as to take into account that the parameters in the list *l* need to be evaluated explicitly. Hence instead of ORF[*l*] we write ORF[*l,a*] and in the second line replace car [*l*] by eval[car[*l*],*a*], and insert a second parameter *a* for the call on ORF

```
         0 1
DEFINE((
     2     3       4    4 4
     (ORF(LAMBDA(L  A)(COND
         5 6        6   5
         ((NULL  L)NIL)
         5 6      7      8    8 7 6 6    7        7 6 5
         ((NULL(EVAL(CAR  L)A))(ORF(CDR  L)A))
         5    5
         (T  T)
     4 3 2
     )))
   1 0
   ))
```

and then

```
DEFLIST((
   (OR(LAMBDA(U  V)(ORF  U  V)))
   )FEXPR)
```

or even

```
DEFLIST(((OR  ORF))FEXPR).
```

One might be tempted to replace directly the ORF function by OR and the DEFINE by DEFLIST but this does not work because of the recursive call on ORF in the body of ORF. If that call were replaced by OR, funny things would naturally happen to its two parameters (CDR L) and A. In general we must never define an FEXPR which calls on itself directly or indirectly but must proceed as above.

Here is a final example: in this there are arbitrarily many variables, some having to be evaluated, and one of them not. Let FF be the FEXPR such that the form

$$(FF \; S_1 \text{—} S_N \; B)$$

is evaluated by evaluating S_1–S_N in turn and yielding the unevaluated B. Thus, e.g.

```
(FF(PRINT X)(PRINT Y)END)
```

would print the value of X and Y and would yield the atom END. Proceeding as above this could be defined by

```
       01
DEFINE((
    2   3       4   44
    (FFF(LAMBDA(X A)(COND
       56     7     766       65
       ((NULL(CDR X))(CAR X))
       5 6   7     8      8 765432
       (T(AUX(EVAL(CAR X)A))))))
    2   3      4 44    5      5 432
    (AUX(LAMBDA(D)(FFF(CDR X)A)))
    10
))

DEFLIST(((FF FFF))FEXPR)
```

Finally we can of course define several FEXPRs using just one DEFLIST e.g.

```
DEFLIST(((FF FFF)(OR ORF))FEXPR).
```

It will be noticed that we have not done anything constructive with the ALIST apart from supplying it to EVAL. I do not know of any applications in which the ALIST is used in some more interesting way. For this reason, in some Lisp systems, EVAL does not have the ALIST parameter, in which case FEXPRs are defined using just one variable. The current ALIST is automatically passed to a call on EVAL. The same applies to the related function APPLY.

If the reader is interested in seeing the current ALIST he can do

```
DEFLIST(((ALIST(LAMBDA(X A)A)))FEXPR)
```

and smuggle into the body of a function G the form

```
(PRINT(ALIST)).
```

When a call on G is being evaluated the current ALIST will then be printed.

6.3 Standard indicators

An atom which is the name of a function defined by DEFINE has the standard indicator EXPR.

If the relevant pair used in defining the function by means of DEFINE is (*atom s*) then *s* will be the property associated with the indicator EXPR in the property list of *atom*. In fact

DEFINE(*list-of-pairs*)

is equivalent to

DEFLIST(*list-of-pairs* EXPR).

We can therefore recover the definition of such a function FN by

GET(FN EXPR)

which is sometimes useful. Similarly

GET(FN FEXPR)

will yield the relevant information for an FEXPR FN. A function of type SUBR or FSUBR has these as indicators. The corresponding properties are not printable but we can do

GET(FN SUBR)

or

GET(FN FSUBR)

to find out whether FN is of one or other of these types. If not, then the answer will be NIL, otherwise some information will be printed. Another standard indicator is APVAL which is placed on the property list of an atom by means of CSET. However,

GET(*atom* APVAL)

will not necessarily yield the corresponding value and is of no interest, since EVAL deals with this.

6.4   RPLACA, RPLACD and the property list of atoms

It is likely, but not certain, that if you type

CDR(B)

{which is illegal} an S-expression will be printed which might look like this:

(PNAME?)

and then, if you type

```
CSET(B(LOLA))
CDR(B)
```

it might print

```
(PNAME ? APVAL((LOLA)))
```

and then, if you type

```
DEFLIST(((B 25))AGE)
CDR(B)
```

it might print

```
(AGE 25 PNAME ? APVAL((LOLA))).
```

What is printed is the CDR of the property list of the atom B, as far as this is possible. The symbol '?' indicates an unprintable item. The CDR of an atom is probably of type

$$(i_1 p_1 i_2 p_2-)$$

where i_1 etc. are 'indicators' and the p_1 etc. the corresponding 'properties'. The CAR of an atom is usually unprintable as it is an 'atom-marker' which indicates to the system that this is the property list of an atom. The property lists of atoms are not usually of interest to the user. They are manipulated behind the scenes by the functions *deflist*, *define*, *get*, *remprop*, *cset*, etc. but the details will only interest an implementer of a Lisp system. For this purpose there are available two 'functions' *rplaca* and *rplacd* which affect the Lisp system in the following way.

A call *rplaca*[x,y] replaces the car[x] by y and thus produces apparently the same as cons[y,cdr[x]] but it does this in a quite different way, i.e. by modifying the S-expression which represents x inside the computer. Thus if, for example, X is a variable bound to some S-expression, then after (RPLACA X Y) X is bound to a different S-expression; this, of course, must not be allowed to happen. The function *rplacd* is similar, *rplacd*[x,y] changes cdr[x] to y, again by modifying the representation of x in the computer, apparently by producing the same as cons[car[x],y].

As a possible application, suppose that the function *remprop* is not available. Assuming z stands for the cdr of an atom x, say

$$z = (i_1 p_1-i_n p_n)$$

then the call *remprop*[*x*,*i*] must remove the pair (*i p*) from *z* if the indicator *i* occurs, otherwise it must leave *z* unaltered. This can be done in a straightforward manner by the function

```
 0          1         2 22      3 4        4      3
(REMOVE(LAMBDA(Z)(COND((NULL  Z)NIL)
   34   5       5 44       43
  ((EQ(CAR  Z)I)(CDDR  Z))
   3 4    5       55     6       66       7         76543
  (T(CONS(CAR  Z)(CONS(CADR  Z)(REMOVE(CDDR  Z)))))
 210
)))
```

and now we need to replace the existing CDR[*x*] by this newly created list. We do this using *rplacd:*

```
(REMPROP(LAMBDA(X  I)(RPLACD  X(REMOVE(CDR  X)))))
```

In the same way any of the others of the property-list functions, *deflist*, etc. may be implemented in this manner, assuming that property lists look as explained above and assuming that they are accessible by means of cdr[*x*].

The functions *rplaca* and *rplacd* and similar functions should not be used for other purposes. One can amuse oneself by typing

```
CSET(V%(C.D))
EVAL((RPLACD  V%  V%)NIL)
```

when surprising things might happen!

Chapter 7

Programs Generating Functions

7.1 Functions yielding functions

Lisp is peculiar in that the language is indistinguishable from the objects on which it operates; they are both expressed as S-expressions. It shares this peculiarity with Church's 'Lambda Calculus'. This has a great theoretical advantage, viz. that the yield of a function call can itself be a Lisp program, or part of one, and in particular the yield can be a function. This is not possible in the more usual programming languages. {Surprisingly even in Algol 68 the following example cannot be imitated}. For example if f_1 and f_2 are functions of one variable their composition {often written $f_{1 \circ} f_2$} is the function g for which $g(x) = f_1(f_2(x))$ {in ordinary mathematical notation}. If F1 and F2 are the corresponding Lisp functions then $f_1(f_2(x))$ is in Lisp the form

```
(LAMBDA(X)(F1(F2 X)))
```

which is a list of the three S-expressions

```
      LAMBDA
      (X)
and   (F1(F2 X)).
```

If we define

```
 0         1      2      2 2       3              3
(COMPOSE(LAMBDA(G1  G2)(LIST(QUOTE  LAMBDA)
     3    4 43
    (QUOTE(X))
     3    4     5       5 4 3
    (LIST G1(LIST G2(QUOTE  X)))
 2 1 0
)))
```

then the call

```
COMPOSE(F1  F2)
```

will yield precisely the above S-expression for $F1_oF2$. In a form the corresponding call would of course be

```
(COMPOSE(FUNCTION F1)(FUNCTION F2))
```

and this form can be used wherever the corresponding function is expected. This type of example accounts for one of our definitions of <form>, i.e. (<form><args>). Here are some further examples:

```
DEFINE((
  COMP(LAMBDA(G1 G2)(COMPOSE G1(COMPOSE G2 G1))))
  (HT(COMPOSE(FUNCTION CAR)(FUNCTION CDR)))
  (NU(LAMBDA(G)((COMP Q% G)(READ))))
))
HT((A B C))
```

{yields} B

```
(COMP(FUNCTION CDR)(FUNCTION REVERSE))((A B C D))
```

{yields} (C B)

```
CSET(Q%(LAMBDA(X)(APPEND(QUOTE(A B C))X)))
```

{yield unimportant}

```
NU(REVERSE)
```

{data} (U V W)
{yields} (A B C W V U C B A)

```
      012    22      22      21
MAPCAR(((I J)(K L M)(U V W))
  1       2              22              210
  (COMPOSE(FUNCTION CDR)(FUNCTION REVERSE)))
```

{yields} ((I)(L K)V U)

The power of this feature is so unusual that it has probably not yet been fully exploited in practice. There are known applications in Artificial Intelligence and in compiler construction.

Here is an alternative way of defining COMPOSE, which uses a quite different idea. Here we do not try to obtain an S-expression which represents a function but use a parameter of type (FUNCTION. . .) and the identify function ID to yield the function:

```
(ID(LAMBDA(Z)Z))
0        1      2      22  3        4          5 5
(COMPOSE(LAMBDA(G1 G2)(ID(FUNCTION(LAMBDA(X)
                                  5  6      6543210
                                  (G1(G2 X)))))))
```

This can be used in the same way as the COMPOSE defined previously. If we look behind the scenes, however, things are quite different. If we call

```
COMPOSE(CAR CDR)
```

we expect to get

```
(LAMBDA(X)(CAR(CDR X)))
```

which indeed would be the yield if the earlier COMPOSE had been used. With the present one the yield is

```
  0    1         2 22  3     32112      223       3210
(FUNARG(LAMBDA(X)(G1(G2 X)))((G2.CDR)((G1.CAR)))))
```

or something similar, depending on the Lisp implementation. This is known as the FUNARG problem and is due to the fact that functional arguments have to be treated in a special way. The above yield is a three-element list of type

```
(FUNARG fn alist)
```

where *fn* represents a function and alist is the association list which contains the relevant information about the values of the variables as they were when the form (FUNCTION *fn*) was evaluated.

7.2 Recursive functions without names

This paragraph is concerned with the following question: what functions can be 'defined' in Lisp without using DEFINE {or the related DEFLIST}? This is called programming in 'pure Lisp'. In this the only function names that may be used are the five primitive functions CAR, CDR, CONS, ATOM, EQ.

If a function *g*, defined by a LAMBDA-expression does not call itself, directly or indirectly, then obviously all occurrences of *g* can be replaced by that LAMBDA-expression. Thus the name G of *g* is, in theory, superfluous, though in practice it may be essential, for obvious reasons of ease of programming and legibility. If, however, *g* calls itself then it seems essential to name *g* and all other functions involved in its definition. Lisp provides the LABEL facility so that even in this case *g* can be replaced by a kind of LAMBDA-expression. For instance, the form (APPEND X Y) can be replaced by

```
 0 1              2          3    33      4 5      5  4
((LABEL APP(LAMBDA(U  V)(COND((NULL  U)V)
  4  5    6      6
  (T(CONS(CAR  U)
    6   7       7 6
    (APP(CDR  U)V)
 54321     0
 )))))X  Y)
```

LABEL gives the function a name during evaluation. Here the name APP is used only during the evaluation of the form and is then forgotten. This facility is not particularly interesting from our point of view and is probably never used in practice {except by those who like it!}. The following will interest students of the theory of computability. Suppose that G is any Lisp function of one variable. It is defined by some expression

(G(LAMBDA(X) B[X,G]))

where $B[X,G]$ stands for some form which in general will contain both X and G explicitly {as well as other function symbols}. If we define M by

(M(LAMBDA(Z U)B[Z,U]))

then G can equally well be defined by

(G(LAMBDA(X)(M X(FUNCTION G))))   {1}

Let us make the following definitions:

```
       0 1
DEFINE((
  2  3      4   44       432
  (YY(LAMBDA(Z  U)(U  Z  U)))
  2 3       4  44     5        5432
  (H(LAMBDA(X)(YY  X(FUNCTION  G1)))))
  2  3      4   44     5
  (G1(LAMBDA(Q  V)(M  Q(FUNCTION
    6       7 77      76543
    (LAMBDA(R)(V  R  V)))))
  2
  )
10
))
```

When Lisp evaluates the form (H W) {where W is a variable bound to some value} it evaluates this as ((Y W(FUNCTION G1)) and this has the value of the form (G1 W(FUNCTION G1)) i.e.

(M W(FUNCTION(LAMBDA(R)(G1 R(FUNCTION G1)))))

which can be written

```
(M W(FUNCTION(LAMBDA(R)(YY R(FUNCTION G1)))))
```

which in turn is

```
(M W(FUNCTION(LAMBDA(R)(H R)))
```

i.e.

```
(M W(FUNCTION H))
```

This proves that the forms (H W) and (M W(FUNCTION H)) have the same value, if any.

Now a function G which satisfies {1} is called a 'fix-point' of M, for obvious reasons. One would of course never define G by {1} unless G is the only function satisfying {1} irrespective of how the evaluation proceeds, i.e. unless G is the only fix-point of M. By the above calculations H is also a fix-point of M and by the supposed uniqueness, H and G are the *same function*. We also note that H, YY and G1 do not call themselves, directly or indirectly. Hence we can replace the definitions of H {or G} by a long LAMBDA-expression {cf. John McCarthy (1963): A basis for a mathematical theory of computation. In *Computer Programming and Formal Systems*, 3, ed. Braffort & Hirschberg, North-Holland Publishing Co.}. The interested reader will easily extend this method to several functions, calling each other, by 'eliminating' their names one at a time, and to functions of more than one variable {which in principle are not actually needed}. Thus, any computation which can be done in Lisp {and therefore anything that is computable} can also be done in 'pure Lisp' {without using LABEL}. The function YY is related to the so-called paradoxical combinations of H.B. Curry; other similar expressions could also be used instead. Thus Lisp lends itself well to the computer verification of some aspects of this theory.

Chapter 8

Debugging

8.1 Detecting and avoiding errors

The syntax of Lisp is so simple that it is difficult for the system to give meaningful error messages. Lisp systems usually offer some tracing facilities, e.g. a function TRACE which is invoked thus:

$$\text{TRACE}((f_1 \ f_2 -))$$

where f_1, f_2 etc. stand for function names. After this call any computation involving these functions will result in copious printing of various details such as the list of arguments used by each function and possibly the yield of the evaluation. This will usually reveal where the first error occurs. Tracing is also interesting as it gives a picture of the whole computation.

Mysterious errors can be due to atoms being used for variables when these atoms have APVALs. This error will be avoided by denoting such atoms in a special way, as we have done, though nothing can be done about built-in atoms such as F,T,LPAR,PERIOD, etc.

Strange things can happen if one defines and uses a function whose name coincides with a built-in function. According to the definition in the *Lisp Manual* this should not matter as a DEFINEd definition should over-ride any other, but in some implementations this is not the case. If one suspects this one can confirm it by using PRINTPROP which will show whether the function atom has the indicators SUBR or FSUBR. One can find all built-in atoms by EVAL(OBLIST NIL). This will print out all atoms known to the system at that point, including all those introduced by the programmer, so this call should be made before anything else.

The most frequent errors are due to wrong bracketing, so bracket counting should always be done, even by the most experienced Lisp user. These errors often manifest themselves by error messages of the type 'too many {or too few} parameters'.

If one uses functions for their side effects e.g. {PRINT}, the yield being unimportant one might be tempted to make them yield NIL or not

68

to worry about the yield at all. This can lead to unexpected difficulties,
e.g. in COND or AND. The best practice here is to make such functions
have some specific non-NIL yield e.g. FINISHED. This will also be
helpful in tracing these functions.

Errors will more easily be found and corrected if one does not use
functions with large, complicated bodies. The methods used in this book
lead naturally to functions with small bodies.

As an example of using *trace*, suppose we want to have a function
which when applied to a list of pairs such as $((a_1\ b_1)(a_2\ b_2)-(a_n\ b_n))$
inverts the pairs, yielding $((b_1\ a_1)(b_2\ a_2)-(b_n\ a_n))$. A beginner in Lisp
might try

```
 0            1       2 22
(NEWPAIRS(LAMBDA(X)(COND
   3 4    5      5 4 4    5       5 5     5 4 3
   ((NULL(CDR X))(LIST(CADR X)(CAAR X)))
   3  4   5    6     6 6      6 5
   (T(CONS(CONS(CADR X)(CAAR X))
     5       6      6 5 4 3
     (NEWPAIRS(CDR X)))))
 2 1 0
 )))
```

which contains several typical errors. We now try it.

```
NEWPAIRS((A1 B1)(A2 B2))
→ ERROR:MISMATCHED LISTS
TRACE((NEWPAIRS))
→ NIL
NEWPAIRS((A1 B1)(A2 B2))
→ ERROR:MISMATCHED LISTS
```

This shows that the error has occurred even before the body of
NEWPAIRS has been entered. There is probably something wrong with
((A1 B1)(A2 B2)). Of course we see now what it should be and type

```
NEWPAIRS(((A1 B1)(A2 B2)))
→ TRACING
→ NEWPAIRS(((A2 B2)))
→ ERROR:EXPECTING A NOTATOM[CADR]
→ TRACEBACK
→ (CADR X)
→ (LIST(CADR X)(CAAR X))
→ (COND
  {etc}
```

This information shows that the trouble occurred in the call
NEWPAIRS(((A2 B2))), so the first pair had given no trouble. It
happened when evaluating (CADR X) which occurred in the form
(LIST(CADR X)(CAAR X)) so possibly something needs changing in
this form. Looking at the problem again we see that (CADR X) should
be (CADAR X) in both places. We modify our function accordingly:

```
 0         1        2 22
(NEWPAIRS(LAMBDA(X)(COND
  34    5     544    5       55      543
  ((NULL(CDR X))(LIST(CADAR X)(CAAR X)))
  3 4   5    6    66       65
  (T(CONS(CONS(CADAR X)(CAAR X))
     5      6     6543
     (NEWPAIRS(CDR X)))))
 210
 )))
```

and then

```
NEWPAIRS(((A1 B1)(A2 B2)))
→ ((B1.A1)B2 A2)
```

which is not what we want. Then

```
TRACE((NEWPAIRS))
→ NIL
NEWPAIRS(((A1 B1)(A2 B2)))
→ TRACING
→ NEWPAIRS(((A2 B2)))
→ YIELD:(B2 A2)
→ ((B1.A1)B2 A2)
```

This shows that NEWPAIRS(((A2 B2))) yields (B2 A2) whereas we
want ((B2 A2)). We see that we need an extra LIST in the function and
try

```
 0         1        2 22
(NEWPAIRS(LAMBDA(X)(COND
  34    5     544    5    6       66      6543
  ((NULL(CDR X))(LIST(LIST(CADAR X)(CAAR X))))
  3 4   5    6    66      65
  (T(CONS(CONS(CADAR X)(CAAR X))
    5      6     6543
    (NEWPAIRS(CDR X))))
 210
 )))
```

and this produces, when the same call as before is made, ((B1.A1)(B2 A2)). The second pair is now correct, the first slightly faulty. We obviously need to replace a CONS by LIST:

```
 0                1       2 22
(NEWPAIRS(LAMBDA(X)(COND
   3 4    5      5 4 4 5   6         6 6      6 5 4 3
   ((NULL(CDR X))((LIST(CADAR X)(CAAR X))))
   3 4   5      6        6 6      6 5
   (T(CONS(LIST(CADAR X)(CAAR X))
      5        6      6 5 4 3
      (NEWPAIRS(CDR X))))
 2 1 0
)))
```

and this is now all right.

8.2 The garbage collector

This is a program which is part of most Lisp systems; it manages the space requirements during computations. It is automatically called when necessary and it usually manifests itself by some message to the user. If there are many such messages during a computation one can conclude that the program requires a lot of computer space. If finally the desired result is produced then all is well, otherwise one can suspect that one is trying to perform a non-terminating computation. Tracing will usually confirm this by showing the same forms being evaluated many times and in the same order.

If after a garbage collection very strange unexpected S-expressions are printed one can suspect a systems fault. If there is such a fault it will probably show up sooner or later after a garbage collection. In that case, doing things in a slightly different order might bypass the fault.

Chapter 9

Miscellaneous Useful Examples

9.1 Quicksort

This well-known algorithm is used for sorting items into ascending {or descending} order. We assume we have a list l of S-expressions {which could be numbers} on which is defined a partial order BEFORE. Thus BEFORE[x,y] is true if and only if $x < y$ in this partial order. The order being partial means that there may be elements x,y in the list such that all of BEFORE[x,y],BEFORE[y,x] and EQUAL[x,y] are false. We wish to obtain a list m containing the same elements as l such that whenever BEFORE[x,y] is true then x comes before y in m. We shall define a function QUICKSORT which when applied to l yields m. It uses SPLIT. SPLIT[s,x] splits the list s into three sublists S_1,S_2,S_3 where S_1 consists of the elements $s' < x$, S_2 consists of the $s'>x$ and S_3 consists of the remaining elements of s. The yield of SPLIT we take as $(S_1\ S_2.S_3)$.

QUICKSORT[l] calls SPLIT[l,car[l]] producing S_1,S_2,S_3 as above, forms l_1 = QUICKSORT[s_1], l_2 = QUICKSORT[s_2] and yields m = append[l_1,append[s_3,l_2]].

Here is a blueprint:

```
split[s,x]::=if s=NIL then (NIL NIL.NIL)
                 else let(u.v)=s;
                       if u < x then auxplit[1]
                       else if u > x then auxplit[2]
                            else auxplit[3]
                            fi
                       fi
                 fi.
auxplit[n]::= let y = split[v,x] = (s₁s₂.s₃) {say}.
{auxplit2[y]} if n=1 then yield((u.s₁)s₂.s₃) {s₁=car[y]}
                 else if n=2 then yield(s₁(u.s₂).s₃) {s₂=cadr[y]}
                      else yield(s₁ s₂.(u.s₃)) {s₃=cddr[y]}
                      fi
                 fi.
```

$$\text{quicksort}[s]::= \textit{if } s=\text{NIL } \textit{then } \text{NIL}$$

$$\textit{else } \text{let } (a.b) = s,$$

$$\text{let } z = \text{split}[s,a]=(s_1 s_2.s_3) \ \{\text{say}\}.$$

$$\{\text{quick}[z]\} \ \text{let } l_1 = \text{quicksort}[s_1], \ \{s_1=\text{car}[z]\}$$

$$l_2 = \text{quicksort}[s_2], \ \{s_2=\text{cadr}[z]\}$$

$$\text{yield } \text{append}[l_1,\text{append}[s_3,l_2]] \ \{s_3=\text{cddr}[z]\}$$

$$\textit{fi}.$$

and the program is as follows

```
        0 1
DEFINE((
2           3          4  44          5        6        6 5432
(AUXPLIT(LAMBDA(N)(AUXSPLIT2(SPLIT(CDR S)X))))
2            3          4  44   56         6
(AUXSPLIT2(LAMBDA(Y)(COND((EQUAL N 1)
  6    7   8     88    877      76556          6
 (CONS(CONS(CAR S)(CAR Y))(CDR Y)))((EQUAL N 2)
  6    7    77    8    9     99     988        8765
 (CONS(CAR Y)(CONS(CONS(CAR S)(CADR Y))(CDDR Y))))
                       5 6    7    77     8         8
                      (T(CONS(CAR Y)(CONS(CADR Y)
   8     9    99     98765
  (CONS(CAR S)(CDDR Y)))))
432
)))
2         3        4   44   56        66
(SPLIT(LAMBDA(S X)(COND((NULL S)(CONS NIL
                                     7        765
                                    (CONS NIL NIL)))
 56        7      7   7 66         65
((BEFORE(CAR S)CAR S)X)(AUXSPLIT 1))
 56        7     766        65
((BEFORE X(CAR S))(AUXSPLIT 2))
 5 6         65
(T(AUXSPLIT 3))
432
)))
2            3        4  44   56      6     5
(QUICKSORT(LAMBDA(S)(COND((NULL S) NIL)
 5 6       7       8      8765
(T(QUICK(SPLIT S(CAR S))))
432
)))
2        3        4  44     5           6      65
(QUICK(LAMBDA(Z)(APPEND(QUICKSORT(CAR Z))
 5       6      66         7       765
(APPEND(CDDR Z)(QUICKSORT(CADR Z)))
432
)))
10
))
```

If for instance the elements are numbers which are to be sorted in ascending order we do

```
DEFINE(((BEFORE LESSP)))
```

and for descending order (BEFORE GREATERP).

9.2   Permutations

Let *start* = (a_1-a_m) where the a_i stand for distinct S-expressions. We wish to generate all permutations of *start*. This means we wish to define an enumeration of all the permutations by means of a function NEXTPERM so that if l is a permutation then NEXTPERM [*start*,*l*] yields the permutation after l in this enumeration, if there is one, otherwise we make it yield FINISHED. Here is the informal skeleton of this program.

nextperm[*start*,*l*]::=   *if* l = NIL *then* FINISHED
                            else let a = car[*l*],
                                       m = cdr[*l*];
{otherwise[*m*]}   *let* start2 be the list obtained
                            from *start* by removing a;
{again1[*start2*]}   *let* l_2 = nextperm[*start2*,*m*];
{again2[l_2]}   *if* l_2 ≠ FINISHED *then* cons[a,l_2]
{again3[a_i]}   *else*
                            if a_i = right neighbour of a in
                            start
                            then cons[a_i,remove a_i from *start*]
                            else FINISHED
                            fi fi fi.

Here is the program

```
       0 1
DEFINE((
2           3      4      4 4     5 6      6 6
(NEXTPERM(LAMBDA(START L)(COND((NULL L)(QUOTE

                                                  6 5
                                            FINISHED))

    5 6        7        7 6 5 4 3 2
    (T(OTHERWISE(CDR L))))))))
2            3        4   4 4    5       6      6     5 4 3 2
(OTHERWISE(LAMBDA(M)(AGAIN1(REMOVE(CAR L)START))))
2       3      4        4 4   5              5 4 3 2
(AGAIN1(LAMBDA(START2)(AGAIN2(NEXTPERM START2 M))))
2      3      4   4 4
(AGAIN2(LAMBDA(L2)(COND
    5 6    7           8                8 7 6 6    7       7   6 5
    ((NULL(EQUAL L2(QUOTE FINISHED))))(CONS(CAR L)L2))
    5 6      7          8       8 7 6 5 4 3 2
    (T(AGAIN3(NEXT START(CAR L))))))))
2       3      4  4 4    5   6        7                    7 6 5
(AGAIN3(LAMBDA(AI)(COND(AI(CONS AI(REMOVE AI START)))
```

```
    5 6            65432
    (T(QUOTE FINISHED))))))
  2     3      4   4 4    5 6      7     7 66      6 5
  (REMOVE(LAMBDA(A  L)(COND((EQUAL(CAR  L)A)(CDR  L))
    5 6   7    77      8      8765432
    (T(CONS(CAR  L)(REMOVE  A(CDR  L))))))))
  2   3      4    4 4    5 6   7     7 6    5
  (NEXT(LAMBDA(S  A)(COND((NULL(CDR  S))NIL)
    5 6     7     7 66      6 5
    ((EQUAL(CAR  S)A)(CADR  S))
    5 6    7     7 65432
    (T(NEXT(CDR  S)A)))))
  1 0
  ))
```

Here is an application of permutations to solving a puzzle which appeared on beer mats in certain pubs: 'At the end of the year all the teams from the various pubs in a local darts league got together . . ..The captains of the top five teams made the following statements:

'Hare and Hounds': "Our pub did not finish fifth."
'Red Lion':   "The 'Green Man' came third."
'Green Man':   "The 'Hare and Hounds' finished lower
                      down the table than the 'George'."
'White Lion':   "The 'George' was second."
'George':   "The 'White Lion' did not win the league."

For some reason, both the captains of the pubs finishing first and second were not telling the truth. The others were. What was the actual finishing order of the league?'

Here we define a function FINDALL so that if *initial* is a permutation of the five pubs FINDALL[*initial*] prints all the permutations which satisfy the above conditions. There is of course only one such permutation. The program is easy to understand.

```
          0 1
  DEFINE((
  2          3      4   4 4
  (MEMBERNUM(LAMBDA(N  L)(COND
    5 6      6 6      6 5 5  6      7         7 7     7 6 5
    ((EQUAL N  1)(CAR  L))(T(MEMBERNUM(SUB1  N)(CDR  L))))
  4 3 2
  )))
  2      3      4     4 4    5 6      7     7 6  5
  (BEFORE(LAMBDA(X  Y  L)(COND((EQUAL Y(CAR  L))NIL)
    5 6     7     7 6 5
    ((EQUAL X(CAR  L))T)
    5 6    7     7 6 5
    (T(BEFORE X  Y(CDR  L)))
  4 3 2
  )))
```

```
²(SAYS³(LAMBDA⁴(X P)⁴⁴(COND
  ⁵⁶((EQUAL X HHX)⁶⁶(NULL⁷(EQUAL⁸(MEMBERNUM 5 P)HH%)⁸)⁷⁶⁵)
  ⁵⁶((EQUAL X RL%)⁶⁶(EQUAL⁷(MEMBERNUM 3 P)GM%)⁷⁶⁵)
  ⁵⁶((EQUAL X GM%)⁶⁶(BEFORE GE% HH% P)⁶⁵)
  ⁵⁶((EQUAL X WL%)⁶⁶(EQUAL GE%⁷(MEMBERNUM 2 P)⁷⁶⁵)
  ⁵⁶((EQUAL X GE%)⁶⁶(NULL⁷(EQUAL WL%⁸(MEMBERNUM 1 P)⁸⁷⁶⁵)
⁴³²)))

²(TEST³(LAMBDA⁴(X P)⁴⁴(COND
  ⁵⁶((OR⁷(EQUAL X⁸(MEMBERNUM 1 P)⁸⁷⁷)(EQUAL X⁸(MEMBERNUM 2
                                               ⁸⁷⁶
                                               P)⁷⁷)
    ⁶(NULL⁷(SAYS X P)⁷⁶⁵⁵)⁶(T ⁶(SAYS X P)⁶⁵)
⁴³²)))

²(EXAMINE³(LAMBDA⁴(P)⁴⁴(COND⁵⁶((EQUAL P⁷(QUOTE FINISHED)⁷⁶)
                                               ⁶(PRINT P)⁶⁵)
  ⁵⁶((SOLN1 P)⁶⁶(AND⁷(PRINT P)⁷⁷(EXAMINE⁸(NEXTPERM INITIAL
                                               ⁸⁷⁶⁵
                                               P)⁸⁷⁶⁵)))
  ⁵⁶(T⁶(EXAMINE⁷(NEXTPERM INITIAL P)⁷⁶⁵)
⁴³²)))

²(FINDALL³(LAMBDA⁴(INITIAL)⁴⁴(EXAMINE INITIAL)⁴³²))
²(SOLN1³(LAMBDA⁴(P)⁴⁴(SOLN2 P P)⁴³²))
²(SOLN2³(LAMBDA⁴(P S)⁴⁴(COND⁵⁶(S⁷(AND⁸(TEST⁸(CAR S)⁸⁷P)
      ⁷(SOLN2 P⁸(CDR S)⁸⁷)
    ⁶⁵))
  ⁵(T P⁵)
⁴³²)))
¹⁰))

CSET(HH% HARE&HOUNDS)

CSET(RL% RED-LION)

CSET(GM% GREEN-MAN)
```

```
CSET(WL% WHITE-LION)

CSET(GE% GEORGE)
```

Now EVAL ((FINDALL(LIST HH% RL% GM% WL% GE%))NIL)
will print the solution.

9.3 Euclid's algorithm

If a and b are positive integers this famous algorithm finds h, the
greatest common divisor of a and b, and (in its modern form) finds
integers x and y such that $ax+by = h$. In the following EUCLID[a,b]
yields the three element list ($h\ x\ y$). DIVIDE, DIFFERENCE, TIMES,
ZEROP are standard functions.

The idea is to divide a by b

$$a = q \times b + r.$$

If $r = 0$ then $h = b, x = 0, y = 1$. If $r \neq 0$ the greatest common divisor of
b and r is also h. Hence, calling euclid[b,r] yields ($h\ u\ v$) where

$$u \times b + v \times r = h$$

so the required x and y are $x = v, y = u - q \times v$ as we see by replacing r
by $a - q \times b$. This gives the blueprint

euclid[a,b]::=let $\ p\ = $ divide[a,b] $ = (q\ r)$ {say}
$\qquad\qquad\qquad\quad${$q\ =$ car[p],$r = $ cadr[p]}.
{eux[p]} $\ $ if $r = 0$ *then* yield $(b\ 0\ 1)$
$\qquad\qquad\quad$*else* let $\ triple\ = $ euclid($b\ r$] $=(h\ u\ v)$, say
$\qquad\qquad\quad${$h\ =$ car[$triple$], $u = $ cadr[$triple$], $v\ =$ caddr
$\qquad\qquad\quad$[$triple$]};{eux2[$triple$]} yield($h\ v\quad u - q \times v$).

```
         0 1
DEFINE((
 2        3       4    4 4    4 5        5 4 3 2
(EUCLID(LAMBDA(A B)(EUX((DIVIDE A B))))
 2     3      4  4 4    5 6      7     7 6 6    6 5
(EUX(LAMBDA(P)(COND((ZEROP(CADR P))(LIST B 0 1))
 5 6   7        8     8 7 6 5
(T(EUX2(EUCLID B(CADR P)))))
4 3 2
)))
 2      3      4       4 4    5         5 5          5
(EUX2(LAMBDA(TRIPLE)(LIST(CAR TRIPLE)(CADDR TRIPLE)
 5           6        6 6    7     7 7          7
 (DIFFERENCE(CADR TRIPLE)(TIMES(CAR P)(CADDR TRIPLE)
6 5 4 3 2
)))))
1 0
))
```

Chapter 10

The Lisp System Re-examined

10.1   Introduction

The Lisp system works in most cases precisely as one expects; very occasionally one might be in some doubt and then one needs to know the exact way in which something is evaluated. Also, cryptic references in Lisp documents to various implementation matters need to be deciphered. I will attempt to explain these matters. There are two mutually recursive functions *eval* and *apply* {*eval* we have already met in Section 4.2}, of two and three variables respectively, in terms of which everything is defined. One therefore needs to know only how these two functions behave. The purpose of *eval* is to evaluate forms, i.e. function 'calls' and this is all there is in Lisp. *Apply* can be regarded as being merely a 'servant' of *eval*; most Lisp systems, however, make it available to the user as it may occasionally prove useful.

10.2   The association list *alist*

We have already seen that *alist* is a list of 'dotted' pairs $((x_1.a_1)$ $(x_2.a_2)–(x_n.a_n))$ in which the x_i are atoms and the a_i are S-expressions. This must be taken literally, for neither x_i nor a_i get *evaluated* inside *alist*; these objects stand for themselves.

During the evaluation of a function call, *alist* changes several times and ends up as it was at the beginning when the evaluation is completed. *Alist* behaves in fact exactly like a 'stack' used in evaluating function calls in other computer languages and it may well be implemented as a stack in Lisp, for it is hidden from the user {except as an aid to 'debugging'}.

If the pair $(x.a)$ occurs in *alist* we say that x is 'bound to a' in *alist* and we call $(x.a)$ a binding of x to a. Here x is a formal parameter of some function {or a *prog* variable} and a is the corresponding actual argument. x may occur several times as the left member of a pair in *alist*, e.g. $(–(x.a)–(x.b)–)$. The binding $(x.a)$ is said to be 'more recent' than $(x.b)$ {because it is further to the left} and of course the left-most pair

78

involving x, say $(x.c)$ is called the 'most recent' binding of x. The tables in Appendix 1 show how evaluation of a form proceeds. The table is used by starting in the top left. When a condition in column 2 is satisfied then we move to the next item on the right, if not then we go to the next item below in column 2. If we get ERROR then the computation is finished with undefined value {an error message should be produced}. A simple example should make this clear.

Let us see how the form

```
(ATOM(HEAD X))
```

is evaluated when the current *alist* is

```
((X.(ABC))—)
```

and HEAD has been defined by

```
DEFINE(((HEAD(LAMBDA(Z)(CAR Z))))).
```

Using the table for *eval*[*form*,*alist*] we have here

$$u = \text{ATOM}\{\text{which is an atom}\} \left.\right\} \qquad \{1\}$$
$$v_1 = (\text{HEAD X}), n=1 \left.\right\}$$

alist is as above, the '—' indicating that the rest (if present) is irrelevant. Since u has indicator SUBR there is a corresponding internal function $u^* = atom^*$ and eval is called upon to get the value v_1^* of v_1. In this case

$$u = \text{HEAD}$$
$$v_1 = \text{X}, \, n=1.$$

u has indicator EXPR {because HEAD has been DEFINEd} so $u^* = $ (LAMBDA(Z)(CAR Z)). The value v_1^* of v_1 is obtained by *eval* from the *alist* since X is an atom not having an APVAL, its value is (A B C). Now *apply*[u^*, ((A B C)),*alist*] is called; apply adds the pair (Z. (A B C)) onto the *alist* which becomes

$$newalist = ((Z.(A \; B \; C))(X.(A \; B \; C))—)$$

and calls *eval*[(CAR Z),*newalist*].

Since CAR is an atom with indicator SUBR this yields car^*[(A B C)]=A,car^* being the relevant internal function. This gives $v_1 = $ A in {1} and now apply[$atom^*$,(A),((X.(A B C))—)] yields finally $^*T^*$.

10.3   The top level

When we type in a pair of S-expressions, say

   fn arglist

at the top level then *fn* is regarded as a function and *arglist* is the list of its actual arguments. The Lisp system 'reads' in this pair, putting it into the computer memory in an appropriate way. Any atoms which occur in the pair are looked at. There is a special list of atoms, called OBLIST, and this is examined as each atom is read in. If an atom is not already in the OBLIST then it is added to it and it remains there until you exit from the system.

Next, the function EVALQUOTE is called to evaluate this call. EVALQUOTE is defined informally thus

   evalquote[*fn*,*arglist*] ::=
       if fn is an atom with indicator FEXPR or FSUBR
       then print[*eval*[*cons*[*fn*,*arglist*], NIL]]
       else print[*apply*[*fn*,*arglist*,NIL]]
   fi.

The pair of S-expressions typed in are the actual arguments for *evalquote*. When this pair has been evaluated and the yield printed then the process is repeated with the next pair, etc. Thus, to write a Lisp interpreter, it is 'only' necessary to program *evalquote* in some suitable language.

10.4   Various Lisp systems

One of the most obvious ways in which Lisp systems differ from the one described above is in the top level. They work in the *eval mode* so instead of typing a pair of S-expressions you type a single form, which is then evaluated by *eval*, with second parameter NIL. Thus, instead of typing CDR((A B C)), you time (CDR(QUOTE(A B C)). The advantage is that this is slightly easier to learn, since there is no special top level; the disadvantage is the extra QUOTE. In *eval mode* we have to write

   (DEFINE(QUOTE((a_1 b_1)....)))

and since DEFINE is the most frequently used function at the top level, such Lisp systems usually provide other forms of this function, e.g. DEF or DEFUN in which the QUOTE is not used, e.g.

   (DEF HEAD(LAMBDA(X)(CAR X)))

or even

```
(DEFUN HEAD(X)(CAR X))
```

in the latter case the LAMBDA being suppressed. Apart from this, such systems work in the same way as described up to here, at least 'in general'. Functions *eval* and *apply* often do not have the *alist* parameter which is tacitly assumed to be the internal *alist* as it is at the moment of computation. Differences also arise in the somewhat rare case of a form (*fn a* . . . .) in which *fn* needs to be evaluated. In some systems such evaluation does not take place automatically, or perhaps only in a restricted way, e.g. only to the extent that *fn* is an atom which has been CSET to a function, in which case that function will be used. One can also get unexpected surprises, for instance I typed {in *eval mode*}

```
(CAR(QUOTE(A.B)))
```

and got the reply

```
A.B  {!}
```

It took some time before I realized the truth: in this system the dot can be part of an atom so one needs to separate the dot by a space from each atom to get the required effect. The dot can also be troublesome when it has to be differentiated from the decimal point.

10.5   Lisp compilers

The Lisp system usually consists of a Lisp interpreter, but the more ambitious systems also incorporate a compiler. The advantage of running a compiled program is the much greater speed of evaluation {ten times faster, or more}. Usually, this works as follows: having defined functions in the usual way, you ask for some, or all of them to be compiled by

```
COMPILE((f₁ f₂-))
```

where $f_1, f_2,-$ are the names of the functions. In some systems you give instead the name of a file which the function definitions are written, which is obviously more convenient in most cases. The compiler then in effect replaces the relevant EXPRs by SUBRs and FEXPRs by FSUBRs and the corresponding properties by internal functions. As far as the user is concerned this should make no difference {apart from the increased speed}. The compiler usually needs extra help from the user as regards shared variables and APVALs. Variables which occur free in a function because they are formal parameters of another function are 'declared' before the compilation is requested, by

> SPECIAL((x_1 x_2−))

APVALs will probably have to be declared by

> COMMON((y_1 y_2−))

though this may also apply to some shared variables of the former type. It is also probable that if one function is compiled then all the other functions which share variables or APVALs with it will have to be compiled also. Unfortunately Lisp compilers are not yet very reliable so one should only run compiled programs after everything has been tested in the interpreted mode.

10.6 Saving programs

A Lisp program, whether partly compiled or not, can usually be saved on a file by

> SAVE(*filename*)

from within the Lisp system.

The effect of this is to put all the relevant computer memory into the file. For example,

```
*  CSET(A% (OK.OK))
→  ((OK.OK))
*  DEFINE((HEAD CAR)(REST CDR)).
→  (HEAD REST)
*  SAVE(FILE1)
→  NIL
*  CSET(B% (U V W))
→   ((U V W))
   etc.
```

On another occasion, without entering the Lisp system, we load FILE1 {how this is done depends on the operating system} and ask for it to run. The result will be that we shall find ourselves in the Lisp system exactly as it was before calling SAVE. It will recognize HEAD, REST and A% but not B%, since SAVE was called before B% was defined. SAVE is a great convenience for large programs, especially if they contain atoms which have been CSET to the result of some long computation {as in Chapter 5}.

10.7 The PROG feature

Suppose that we wish to write a function *pi* so that *pi*[n] is the number of primes not exceeding *n* and we have a predicate *prime* so that *prime*[k] is true if and only if *k* is a prime. In a conventional programming language this could be done roughly as follows:

$$
\begin{aligned}
&\textit{integer procedure } pi(n);\\
&\quad\quad \textit{Begin}\\
&\quad\quad \textit{integer } p,n;\\
&\quad\quad \textit{if } n=1 \ \textit{then } pi:=0\\
&\quad\quad \textit{else } p:=0;\\
&\quad\quad \textit{for } m \ \textit{from } 1 \ \textit{to } n \ \textit{do}\\
&\quad\quad\quad\quad \textit{if } \text{prime}(m) \ \textit{then } p:=p+1 \ \textit{fi}\\
&\quad\quad\quad\quad\quad\quad\quad\quad\quad\quad\quad od;\\
&\quad\quad pi:=p\\
&\quad\quad \textit{fi}\\
&\quad\quad \textit{End}
\end{aligned}
$$

Our methods would give the following Lisp analogue

```
 0  1       2 22    3 4         4 3
(PI(LAMBDA(N)(COND((EQUAL N 1)0)
   3 4      4 4    5  6     6 5 4 3
  ((PRIME N)(ADD1(PI(SUB1 N)))))
   3 4  5     5 4 3
  (T(PI(SUB1 N)))
2 1 0
)))
```

Now in evaluating, say, *pi*[200], it will need to evaluate the form (PI 199) and this again requires (PI 198) etc. Each call on PI will create the pair (N.n) and attach it to the *alist* {see Section 10.2} which in the end will look like this:

((N.1)(N.2)—(N.199)(N.200)—)

and for large N we could soon exhaust the available space. On the other hand, the *integer procedure pi(n)* will require only very little space and that space requirement is independent of *n*.

Chapter 10

The loop *for m–do–od*, which occurs there, can also be rendered more primitively as

> *m:=0;*
> L: *m:=m+1;* if prime(*m*) *then p:=p+1 fi;*
> *if m < n then* go to L *fi;*

Lisp provides an FSUBR called PROG which enables one to write such iterative loops, with assignments to variables, thus saving much space and time, at the cost of introducing a construct which is quite foreign to the whole concept of Lisp. Using this, the above could be written as follows:

```
       0 1
DEFINE((

   2   3          4  4 4      5     5
   (PI(LAMBDA(N)(PROG(P M)
       5    6 7           7 7          7 6 5
       (COND((EQUAL  N  1)(RETURN  0)))
       5      5
       (SETQ  P  0)
       5      5
       (SETQ  M  0)
      5      6       6 5
   L  (SETQ  M(ADD1  M))
       5    6 7       7 7       8       8 7 6 5
       (COND((PRIME  M)(SETQ  P(ADD1  P))))
       5    6 7        7 7      7 6 5
       (COND((LESSP  M  N)(GO  L)))
       5        5
       (RETURN  P)
       5
       )
      4 3 2
      )))
   1 0
   ))
```

The atoms P,M which occur in the list (P M), followng PROG, are called the *prog* variables. Next comes a sequence of forms or atoms {the only atom in this sequence here is L}. The atoms act as 'labels' and the form (GO L) has the obvious effect. The form (COND–)is unusual in that it contains only one pair. This is allowed here because if none of the conditions is satisfied {here (EQUAL N 1)} then the form (COND–) inside PROG yields NIL, rather than an error. The form (PROG–) is evaluated by evaluating in turn, each of the forms in it, from left to right, except in so far as (GO<label>) redirects evaluation to another point. When there are no forms left to be evaluated, the PROG form yields NIL, otherwise it yields the value of the first form (RETURN–) which it evaluates. More precisely the form is

(PROG l f_1-f_n)

where l is a list {possibly empty} of atoms, the *prog* variables, and the f_i are forms, including special *prog* forms. The special *prog* forms are of the followng types:

(i) a non-numeric atom, called a label.

(ii) (GO *label*) where *label* is a label which must occur as one of the f_i {and not inside an f_i}.

(iii) (SETQ x y) or (SET(QUOTE x)y) {which are equivalent} where x is an atom, y a form.

(iv) (RETURN f) where f is a form.

(v) Another *prog* form.

(vi) (COND–)

(RETURN f) is evaluated by evaluating f. Its value is the yield of the *prog* form and the evaluation of the *prog* form is thereby completed.

The forms in (iii) are evaluated by binding x on the *alist* to the value of y. When a new (SETQ x z) with the same x is to be evaluated the binding of x is changed on the *alist* so that the previous binding is lost. Usually x is a *prog* variable. Before the form f_1 is evaluated the *prog* variables are put on the *alist*, bound to NIL. Thus the *prog* variables have value NIL until this is changed by SETQ. When the evaluation of the *prog* form is completed the *prog* variables are removed from the *alist*. If an f_i is another *prog* form then its *prog* variables are regarded as quite distinct from the *prog* variables in the list l even if they are represented by the same atom.

The form in (vi) will be of type

(COND(u_1 v_1)–(u_n v_n))

as usual except that the v_i may also be special *prog* forms, including (GO *label*), which has the obvious effect, and as stated before, the u_i may all yield NIL in which case the whole (COND–) yields NIL.

Here is another example. In Section 3.1 the function REV is defined; using PROG it can be defined so

```
0   1         2 22     3     3
(REV(LAMBDA(X)(PROG(Y  Z)
      2    4 5          5 5           5 4 3
   A (COND((NULL  X)(RETURN  Y)))
      3     4     4 3
      (SETQ  Z(CAR  X))
      3    4 5        5 5     5 4 3
      (COND((ATOM  Z)(GO  B)))
      3    4      4 3
      (SETQ  Z(REV  Z))
```

```
      3       4        4 3
   B (SETQ Y(CONS Z Y))
      3       4      4 3
     (SETQ X(CDR X))
      3    3
     (GO A)
 2 1 0
 )))
```

Notice that this still contains a 'recursive' call (REV Z) but another recursive call has been eliminated by the use of PROG.

The Lisp beginner should not use the PROG form as it can lead to very bad habits.

Appendix 1

eval[*form*,*alist*]

form is	Condition	Yield
NIL		NIL
A number		*form* {the number}
An atom	The atom has an APVAL {obtained by cset [*form*,*value*]}	The corresponding value.
An atom	The atom {is a variable} has a binding on *alist*.	If the most recent binding of atom a is $(a.v)$ the yield is v.
	ERROR	
(QUOTE *f*)	*f* is an S-expression	*f*
(QUOTE *f*)	ERROR	
(FUNCTION *f*) {formally this is not a form, but is treated by eval nevertheless.}	*f* is an S-expression	(FUNARG *f* *alist*)
(FUNCTION *f*)	ERROR	
(COND *f*)	*f* is a sequence $(u_1\ v_1)(u_2\ v_2)-$ of one or more pairs of forms.	u_1 is evaluated using *alist*. Let u_1^* be its value {i.e. $u_1^* =$ eval[u_1,*alist*]}. If $u_1^* \neq$ NIL then the yield is $v_1^* =$ eval[v_1,*alist*]. If $u_1^* =$ NIL the pair $(u_2\ v_2)$ is considered, etc.
(COND *f*)	ERROR	ERROR if all u_i have value NIL.
$(uv_1\ v_2 - v_n)$	u is an atom $v_1, -v_n$ are \<args\>s, $n \geqslant 0$. u has indicator EXPR, corresponding property u^* {a function}.	If v_i^* is the value of v_i i.e. $v_i^* =$ eval[v_i,*alist*] the yield is $u^*[v_1^*, -, v_n^*]$, more precisely, apply $[u^*, (v_1^*\ v_2^*-), alist)]$.

Appendix 1

eval[*form*,*alist*]—*contd.*

form is	Condition		Yield
$(uv_1 \, v_2{-}v_n)$	u is an atom $v_1,{-}v_n$ are \<args\>s, $n \geqslant 0$.	u has indicator FEXPR, correspondi-ng property u^* {a function of 2 variables}.	The yield is $u^*[v_1v_2{-}v_n),alist]$ {i.e. apply $[u^*,((v_1v_2{-} v_n),alist),alist]$}.
$(uv_1 \, v_2{-}v_n)$	u is an atom $v_1,{-}v_n$ are \<args\>s, $n \geqslant 0$.	u has indicator SUBR.	Yield as for EXPR but with u^* an internal function.
$(uv_1 \, v_2{-}v_n)$	u is an atom $v_1,{-}v_n$ are \<args\>s, $n \geqslant 0$.	u has indicator FSUBR.	Yield as for FEXPR with with u^* an internal function.
$(uv_1 \, v_2{-}v_n)$	u is an atom $v_1,{-}v_n$ are \<args\>s, $n \geqslant 0$.	u has a binding on *alist*.	Let $(u.u^*)$ be the most recent binding of u. The yield is then $eval[(u^*v_1{-}v_n),alist]$
$(uv_1 \, v_2{-}v_n)$	u is an atom $v_1,{-}v_n$ are \<args\>s, $n \geqslant 0$.	ERROR	
$(uv_1 \, v_2{-}v_n)$	u is not an atom {usually a λ-expression}.		Let v_i^* be the value of v_i {as in EXPR case}. The yield is $u[v_1^*,{-},v_n^*]$ i.e. apply $[u,(v_1^* v_2^*{-}),alist]$.

apply[*fn*,*args*,*alist*]

fn is	Condition	Yield
NIL		NIL
An atom	*fn* has indicator EXPR	Let *fn** be the corresponding property {name of a function or λ-expression}. Yield = apply[*fn**, *args*,*alist*].
An atom	*fn* has indicator SUBR	Let *fn** be the corresponding internal function. Yield = *fn**[*args*] using *alist*. {This is inevitably a little vague}.
An atom	*fn* is bound on *alist*	Let (*fn*,*fn**) be the most recent binding of *fn*. Yield = apply[*fn**,*args*,*alist*]
An atom	ERROR	
(LABEL *name u*)	*name* is an atom, *u* is an S-expression	Let *alist** = ((*name*.*u*).*alist*). Yield = apply[*u*,*args*,*alist**]
(LABEL *name u*)	ERROR	
(FUNARG *u al*)	*u* is an S-expression representing a function, *al* is an association list.	Yield = apply[*u*,*args*,*al*]
(FUNARG *u al*)	ERROR	
(LAMBDA *lf fm*)	*lf* is a (possibly NIL) list of atoms, *fm* is a form. {This is the most usual case}	if *lf* = (x_1–x_n) and *args* = (a_1–a_n), let $alist_1$* = ((x_1.a_1)–(x_n.a_n)), *alist** = append[$alist_1$*,alist]. Yield = eval[*fm*,alist*]
(LAMBDA *lf fm*)	ERROR	
{other}	{the function *fn* needs to be evaluated before it can be used}	Let *fn** = eval[*fn*,*alist*]. Yield = apply[*fn**,*args*,*alist*]

Appendix 2

Some Standard Functions, etc.

Functions used mainly at the top level (excluding compiler functions)

CSET(x y) The atom x is 'assigned' the value y by placing the indicator APVAL on the property list of x and the property (y). The yield is (y).

DEFINE(x) $x = ((a_1 \ e_1)(a_2 \ e_2)-)$; the atom a_i becomes the name of the function e_i; the property list of a_i is given the indicator EXPR and the property e_i. If such an indicator and property were already present they are first removed. The yield is $(a_1 \ a_2-)$.

DEFLIST(x i) $x = ((a_1 \ p_1)(a_2 \ p_2)-)$; i is an atom. This gives the property list of atom a_j the indicator i and property p_j. The yield is $(a_1 \ a_2-)$. Any property already associated with i is first removed.

PRINTPROP(x) This prints all indicators of atom x and corresponding properties. Probably yields NIL.

REMPROP(x i) If the indicator i is on the property list of atom x it is removed together with the corresponding property. Probably yields NIL.

TRACE(x) $x = (u_1 \ u_2-)$, the u_i being the names of functions to be traced.

UNTRACE(x) $x = (u_1 \ u_2-)$, the u_i being the names of functions no longer to be traced.

In the following, all arguments in the forms are evaluated and remarks concerning the arguments refer to their values, unless the contrary is stated. All are SUBRs unless the contrary is stated. $(fn \ x_1 \ x_2-)$ indicates an arbitrary number of arguments.

Functions for creating S-expressions with arguments which need not be lists

(CAR x) x must not be an atom {p. 7}

(CDR x) x must not be an atom {p. 7}

(C–R x) The '–' indicates an arbitrary number of letters 'A' and 'D' in any order. x must not be an atom. {p. 18}

90

(**CONS** *x y*) Yields (*x.y*) {p. 7}
(**LIST** *x₁ x₂–*) {**FSUBR**} Yields (*x₁ x₂–*) {a list} {p. 16}
(**SUBST** *x y z*) Every occurence of the S-expression *y* in *z* is replaced by S-expression *x*.

Functions for creating lists from lists

(**APPEND** *x y*) If *x* = (*a₁–aₘ*), *y* = (*b₁–bₙ*) yields (*a₁–aₘ b₁–bₙ*).
(**MAP** *x* (**FUNCTION** *g*)) If *x* = (*a₁ a₂–*) and *g* is a function of one variable then *g*[(*a1 a₂–*)], *g*[(*a₂ a₃–*)] etc. are evaluated in turn, and the yield is NIL.
(**MAPCAR** *x* (**FUNCTION** *g*)) If *x* = (*a₁ a₂–*) and *g* is a function of one variable then the yield is (*g*[*a₁*] *g*[*a₂*]–).
(**MAPLIST** *x* (**FUNCTION** *g*)) If *x* = (*a₁ a₂–*) and *g* is a function of one variable the yield is (*g*[(*a₁ a₂–*)] *g*[(*a₂–*)]–).
(**PAIR** *x y*) IF *x* = (*a₁ a₂ aₙ*), *y* = (*b₁ b₂–bₙ*) the yield is ((*a₁.b₁*)(*a₂.b₂*)–).
(**REVERSE** *x*) If *x* = (*a₁ a₂–aₙ*) the yield is (*aₙ–a₂ a₁*).

General predicates

(**AND** *x₁ x₂–*) {**FSUBR**} The *xᵢ* are evaluated from left to right until a NIL value is found in which case the yield is NIL, otherwise the yield is *T*.
(**ATOM** *x*) Yields *T* if *x* is an atom, NIL otherwise.
(**EQ** *x y*) At least one of *x,y* should be an atom. May not work for numbers. Yields *T* if *x* and *y* are the same atom, NIL otherwise.
(**EQUAL** *x y*) Yields *T* if *x* and *y* are the same S-expression, NIL otherwise. {Works for numbers also.}
(**MEMBER** *x y*) Yields *T* if *y* = (*a₁ a₂–*) and *x* is one of the *aᵢ*, NIL otherwise.
(**NOT** *x*) and (**NULL** *x*) These are equivalent. Yield *T* if *x* is NIL, NIL otherwise.
(**NUMBERP** *x*) Yields *T* if *x* is a number, NIL otherwise.
(**OR** *x₁ x₂–*) The *xᵢ* are evaluated from left to right until a non-NIL value is found in which case the yield is *T*, otherwise NIL.

Arithmetic functions

(**ADD1** *x*) Yields *x* + 1.

(DIFFERENCE x y**)** Yields $x - y$.

(DIVIDE x y**)** Division with remainder for integers x,y: $x = q \times y + r$ where r is the remainder, the yield is $(q\ r)$.

(MINUS x**)** Yields $-x$.

(PLUS x_1 x_2–**)** Yields $x_1 + x_2 + \ldots$.

(QUOTIENT x y**)** If x and y are integers yields the quotient q defined under DIVIDE, for real numbers yields x/y.

(REMAINDER x y**)** If x and y are integers yields the remainder r defined under DIVIDE.

(SUB1 x**)** Yields $x - 1$.

(TIMES x_1 x_2–**)** Yields $x_1 \times x_2 = \ldots$.

Arithmetic predicates

(EQUAL x y**)** Yields *T* if $x = y$, NIL otherwise. For real numbers it will depend on how near x is to y.

(GREATERP x y**)** Yield *T* if $x > y$, NIL otherwise.

(LESSP x y**)** Yields "T* if $x < y$, NIL otherwise.

(MINUSP x**)** Yields *T* if $x < 0$, NIL otherwise.

(ONEP x**)** Yields *T* if $x = 1$, NIL otherwise. For real numbers this depends on how near x is to 1.

(ZEROP x**)** Yields *T* if $x = 0$, NIL otherwise. For real numbers this depends on how near x is to 0.

PROG functions

(GO L) {FSUBR} L is a label {it is not evaluated}

(RETURN x**)** x is the yield of the PROG form, and evaluation of the form is terminated.

(SET x y**)** The variable x is assigned the value y {x is evaluated}.

(SETQ x y**)** {FSUBR} Equivalent to (SET(QUOTE x)y).

'Illegal' functions

In the following functions the argument x, or rather its representation in the computer memory, is replaced by the stated yield.

(NCONC x y**)** Yields (APPEND x y)

(RPLACA x y**)** Yields (CONS y(CDR x)).

(RPLACD x y**)** Yields (CONS(CAR x)y).

Input and output

(PRIN1 *x***)** Prints the atom *x*. Leaves printing device on the same line. Yields *x*.

(PRINT *x***)** {(WRITE X) or something similar should be available. This is like (PRINT X) but the printing head is not moved to a new line at the end.} Prints the S-expression *x*, then puts printing device onto the next line. Yields *x*.

(READ) Yields the next S-expression (at the top level) which the reading device 'reads'.

(TERPRI) Positions the printing device on the next line, yields NIL.

Property list functions not usually used at top level

(CSETQ *x y***)** {FSUBR} Is equivalent to (CSET(QUOTE *x*)*y*).

(GET *x y***)** If the atom *x* has indicator *y* then it yields the corresponding property, otherwise NIL. *x* and *y* are first evaluated.

APVALs

BLANK Yields one space.
COMMA Yields one comma.
EOF Yields 'end of file' character.
EOR Yields 'end of line' character.
F Yields NIL.
LPAR Yields (.
NIL Yields NIL.
OBLIST Yields list of all atoms present.
PERIOD Yields a dot.
RPAR Yields).
T Yields *T*.

Index